THE LIFE OF DAVID

MICHAEL L. GOWENS

Sovereign Grace Publications
Lexington, Kentucky

The Life of David
Published by Sovereign Grace Publications
Post Office Box 23514
Lexington, KY 40523-3514
www.sovgrace.net
sgpublications@insightbb.com

Copyright © 2011 by Michael L. Gowens
All rights reserved. No portion of this book may be reproduced, stored in a retrieval system, or transmitted in any form or by any means, except for brief quotations in printed reviews, without written permission from the publisher.

ISBN 978-1-929635-11-5

Scripture quotations are from the *King James Version* of the Bible.

Printed in the United States of America.

CONTENTS

Preface	
Introduction	1
Part 1 – David's Ascent to the Throne	
1. Saul's Tragic Decline	7
2. The Unfolding of Divine Providence	13
3. God's Giant, Israel's Champion	21
4. Passions in the Palace	27
5. The Swallow Seeking a Nest	33
6. Covenant Loyalty	39
7. David Stumbles	43
8. Misery's Company	47
9. God, Our Shield & Defender	51
10. God Avenges His Servants	55
11. Divine Restraint	59
12. The Closing of a Chapter	63
13. David's Spiritual Vacuum	67
14. The End of the Road for Saul	71
15. In the Ruins of Ziklag	73
16. Tell it Not in Gath	79
Part 2 – The Glory Years	
17. A Turbulent Transition to the Throne	85
18. Coronation Day	89
19. Recovering the Lost Ark	93
20. The House that God Builds	99
21. David the Great	103
22. Kings, Cripples & Kindness	107
23. Play the Man!	111
Part 3 – Turmoil in David's House	
24. David's Desecration	117
25. Thou Art The Man!	121
26. Reaping the Whirlwind	127
27. Absalom Stole the Hearts	131
28. In the Valley of Humiliation	137
29. The Rebellion Put Down by God	143

30. Coming Home 149
31. Yet Another Revolt 155
32. The Justice of David's God 159
33. Dwelling in the House of the Lord Forever 167

Preface

In contrast to a commentary, an expository essay is an attempt to crystallize the content of a passage for homiletical use. This approach requires the discipline of Biblical exegesis, preserving the integrity and meaning of the passage, but does not offer the scholastic benefit of a detailed analysis such as one would typically find in an exegetical digest or commentary.

As a preacher, however, I prefer this format to the more technical format of a commentary, by virtue of its capacity to display the "big picture" or *telos* of a passage of Scripture. I also believe this format to be more accessible to the average Bible student.

Academics and theologians, in other words, may not find as much as they had hoped is my essay-approach, so far as technicalities of language study and a thorough discussion of the various theological nuances associated with a particular issue is concerned. But I suspect the person in the pew will find this style very readable and helpful.

I am indebted in this work to a number of sources on the life of David, primarily to the late Frederich W. Krummacher's work entitled *David: King of Israel*, A. W. Pink's title *The Life of David*, and Alfred Edersheim's classic volume *Old Testament Bible History*. Each has been very helpful to this study and is recommended to the reader for further reading.

May God use these pages to reignite the passion in our own lives to be men and women "after God's own heart."

Michael Gowens
November 2011

Introduction

God gave us stories. From earliest childhood, most of us have listened to these stories with fascination and delight.

Even today, these stories speak to the depths in our souls, teaching us in real-life terms great truths about the faithfulness and power of God, the tragedy and sorrow of man's disobedience, and the glory and beauty of God's mercy and grace.

These Biblical narratives challenge us to believe God completely and to serve God with new determination as they show us how the Lord worked in the lives of real people just like us. I, for one, am happy that the Bible was not written in the abstract terms of an instruction manual or academic textbook, but in the concrete terms of human experience. How thankful we should be that our Heavenly Father has given us stories!

Through these stories of faith and courage, the characters of the Bible spring to life. Elbert Hubbard said, "Biography broadens the vision and allows us to live a thousand lives in one."

The life of David is a classic example. I know of nothing that stimulates me to greater levels of godliness like the example of uncommon devotion, love, spiritual-mindedness, commitment, and integrity of one of the spiritual "giants." David certainly qualifies, for he is the only character given the precious title "a man God's own heart."

Of all the characters in the Bible, none receives as much attention as David. At least forty-one chapters of Old Testament historical narrative are devoted by the Holy Spirit in order to paint the dramatic portrait of David's life.

He is mentioned in Hebrews 11 in the roll-call of the faithful.

Beside Abraham and Moses, David is the most famous and illustrious figure in Jewish history. He served his own generation by the will of God with such unparalleled devotion that he became the standard by which all subsequent kings were measured (1 Kings 11:4). Who was this "man after God's own heart"?

C. S. Lewis said, "Every man's life consists of a limited number of themes." The themes of David's interesting life are basically five.

First, *David the shepherd* teaches us about godly character. In the quietness of Bethlehem's hills, God trained a young man for public leadership. It was there, in the unpretentious life of protecting the flock from predators and providing for the needs of his lambs that David learned faithfulness and integrity. It was there that God developed within him a servant's spirit.

Secondly, *David the soldier* teaches us about faith in God and courage for God. David was called by God to fight the Lord's battles. Perhaps he would have preferred to live his days in the obscurity of the pastoral scenes that characterized his youth, but God had a more public work for this impressive youth. David was thrust into some very dangerous situations. He exhibited, however, uncommon valor and bravery, for he trusted wholly in the Lord.

Thirdly, *David the singer* teaches us about fellowship with God and spiritual-mindedness. The book of Psalms, a collection of his Divinely inspired poetry for use in the worship of God, is a legacy to his spirituality. David knew how to worship. His life was not only a life of integrity and conflict; it was supremely a life of praise.

Fourth, *David the sovereign* (king) teaches us about honor and responsibility, about serving God by serving his people. It is in this regal glory as the King of Israel that David also prefigures the Lord Jesus Christ, whom God would raise up to sit upon David's throne forever as "King of kings and Lord of lords."

Finally, *David the sinner* teaches us about the tragic consequences of personal failure and the absolute necessity of ongoing diligence to mortify the old nature. David was an outstanding man, but he was not a perfect man.

J. C. Ryle wrote, "The best of men are only men at their very best. Patriarchs, prophets, and apostles—martyrs, fathers, reformers, puritans—all, all are sinners, who need a Savior: holy useful, honorable in their place, but sinners after all."

David was, indeed, a great sinner. But he was also the great penitent, as Psalm 51 demonstrates. God extended great grace to David and in this, David has a message for all of us. Perhaps in his penitence more than anything else, he was "a man after God's own heart."

Part 1

David's Ascent to the Throne

1 Samuel 8 – 2 Samuel 1

Chapter 1
Saul's Tragic Spiritual Decline
1 Samuel 8-15

Just as a jeweler employs the contrast of a dark background to display the brilliance of a precious gem, so the Holy Spirit frames David's illustrious reign over Israel in the context of Saul's self-will and disobedience. Saul's life and reign is a case study in spiritual declension.

The history of his rise to power and subsequent fall, therefore, not only serves to highlight the story of David, but also stands as a powerful practical example of the consequences of departing from the Lord.

"Make us a king"- 1 Samuel 8

Israel was, since its inception, a theocracy (Is. 33:22; Ps. 89:18). God was the absolute monarch in Israel.

In 1 Samuel 8, however, the people renounced reliance on Jehovah as their King by demanding a human regent from Samuel. Why did they make such a request?

(1) Because of a crisis in leadership - As Samuel aged, his sons assumed increasingly more and more responsibility as judges over the people. They, however, were not godly men. Enemy oppression was heavy. Further, this failure of spiritual leadership compounded the general lawlessness that had prevailed for over 500 years since Joshua's death (Jud. 21:25).

(2) Because of peer pressure - The Israelites wanted to be "like the other nations". They were tired of being different. They wanted to conform to popular standards.

At first, Samuel felt personally slighted, but God reminded him, "They have not rejected you, but Me." Their request was essentially a revolt against theocratic rule and a choice for man instead of God. Tired of walking by faith, they wanted to walk by sight.

After taking their complaint before the Lord in prayer, Samuel protested that their king would enlist their children in his army, requisition their property for the government, and tax their substance for his treasury. Still they demanded "We will have a king." The Lord acquiesced to their desire, but He remained sovereign and supreme, even over the king (1 Sam. 12:14-15, 25).

Friedrich Krummacher, a German preacher and author (1796-1868), writes, "God gave them a king in anger [cf Hos. 13:1], but if they, with childlike trust, had allowed Him to do toward them as He pleased, He would one day have given them one in mercy."[1]

That it was God's intention to give them a king at length anyway is clear from 1 Samuel 2:10. Their timing, however, was not His, nor were their motives.

Head and Shoulders Above the Rest (1 Sam. 9-11)

The portrait of Saul painted at the beginning of his reign is impressive. He was a courageous, humble, and immensely talented young man. Well-endowed with both physical beauty and personal charisma, Saul was the people's choice.

He came from a wealthy family. He was also eloquent before crowds. These natural talents had the potential to either become great assets or tremendous liabilities. It depended on the choices he made.

At first, it appeared that he made the right choices. The first indication of his character suggests that Saul was humble (1 Sam. 9:21), "little in his own eyes" (1 Sam. 15:17). At the public inauguration ceremony at Mizpeh,

Saul hid himself among the stuff [lit. baggage] (1 Sam. 10:22).

After his anointing by Samuel, God gave him "another heart." He had holy thoughts, grand resolve, and resolute determination. He even prophesied so that the people wondered, "Is Saul also among the prophets?" Without a doubt, Saul was very unique. He stood out in the crowd - "there was none like him among all the people" (10:24).

God placed his endorsement on Saul by giving him victory over the Ammonites at Jabesh-gilead (1 Sam. 11). There he distinguished himself for bravery and loyalty to his people. He also refused to accept credit for the victory, attributing their success to Jehovah alone (11:13). This military conquest silenced the last of the critics, and prompted Samuel to lay aside his as office as Judge once and for all (1 Sam. 12).

A Tragic Compromise

For two years, Saul reigned with integrity. First Samuel 13, however, records the beginning of the end of his royal career. Here he displays the decaying spirituality in his own heart.

A new crisis against Israel's archenemy, the Philistines, was precipitated when Jonathan attacked the Philistine garrison at Gilgal. As he waited for Samuel to arrive, Saul became impatient. Sensing that he was losing control of the people and that morale was faltering, Saul usurped the role of the priest and offered the burnt offering to the Lord.

Immediately, Samuel arrived and confronted him with the question, *"What hast thou done?"* Instead of acknowledging his presumptuous sin in contrition and repentance, Saul rationalized his behavior. The situation demanded the action, he argued.

By this reckless act under the guise of piety, Saul demonstrated that he was willing to obey God only so long as God's commandments did not cross his self-will. To Saul, "the end justifies the means" (i.e. situation ethics).

He also displayed on this occasion an inappropriate concern for his own reputation: *"The people were scattered from me."* Saul, in other words, was serving Saul, not Jehovah.

Samuel replied, *"Thou hast done foolishly...now thy kingdom shall not continue: the Lord hath sought him a man his own heart, and the Lord hath commanded him to be captain over his people, because thou hast not kept that which the Lord commanded thee"* (1 Sam. 13:13-14).

Again, Saul displayed his own lack of judgment and spirit of self-interest by forbidding food to the soldiers until the enemy was conquered (1 Sam. 14). Had it not been for the people, whose opinion was so important to Saul, Jonathan, who had not heard his father's oath, would have died for tasting a little honey (14:44-45).

Saul soon disobeyed again in reference to the command to "utterly slay" the Amalekites (1 Sam. 15). In the confrontation that followed, Saul discloses his real motivation: *"I feared the people."*

Even after Samuel repeated the dreaded refrain, *"God hath rejected thee from being king"* Saul was more concerned to preserve his reputation in the eyes of the people than he was in repentance before God: *"Turn again with me...honor me now, I pray thee, before the elders of my people, and before Israel..."* (1 Sam. 15:25, 30).

Krummacher comments, "Here we see, then, his deepest thoughts disclosed before us. Instead of being filled with repentance before God, he is only concerned with his honor among men."[2] After that, Samuel *"sought no more after Saul."*

The ruin of King Saul began in his own heart. Slowly and imperceptibly, Saul forgot his Divine commission. Motivated not by a sense of his calling but by his own proud ambition and self-concern, Saul became a "driven" man.

The Lord only uses "called" men. He avoids those who are driven by their own agenda and want to use Him. In his book *Ordering Your Private World*, Gordon MacDonald depicts Saul as the classic driven man.

"When Saul became king of Israel," MacDonald writes, "he enjoyed too much immediate success. It apparently made him unaware that he had any limits to his life. He spent little time pondering his need for others, engendering a relationship with God, or even facing his responsibilities toward the people over whom he ruled...he saw himself as being too important."[3] Saul got a taste of power and, like an infant with a stick of candy, would not let it go.

Remarkably, Saul sat on the throne another 38 years, but they were marked by a dark brow, a haunting spiritual emptiness and vacuum, and an embittered heart. God had departed from Saul, for Saul had departed from the Lord.

---

[1] F. W. Krummacher, *David: King of Israel*, p. 17
[2] Krummacher, p. 21
[3] Gordon MacDonald, *Ordering Your Private World*, p.15

Chapter 2
The Unfolding of Divine Providence
1 Samuel 16

First Samuel 16 may be divided into two parts: (1) David Anointed by Samuel (vs. 1-13); (2) David Brought into Saul's Court (vs. 14-23).

Like so many Old Testament narratives, the theme of Divine providence is skillfully, yet implicitly, woven into the fabric of this narrative.

Providence means that, in the words of Isaac Watts, "He rules the world with truth and grace." God is not passively indifferent to the lives of His children, but watches over all, beholding the evil and the good.

At times, he directly intervenes to accomplish his purpose either by orchestrating circumstances—as He did when he sent the plagues on Egypt for the sake of convincing them to let His people go—and sometimes by overruling circumstances intended to harm His people for the sake of their protection—as He did in the story of Haman's plot to exterminate the Jews in Esther's day. It is because we believe in Providence that Christians talk about the importance of living by faith and trusting in the Lord.

Though the surface details of 1 Samuel 16 mention nothing of "providence," the invisible hand of God is carefully guiding and directing David's life, overruling the unfolding of circumstances to accomplish His will. God intended to make David the king of Israel and the details of how that intention would become reality now begin to unfold in a remarkable way.

Samuel's Fear (vs. 1-5)

"And the Lord said to Samuel, How long wilt thou mourn for Saul, seeing I have rejected him from reigning over Israel... " (v. l) Change is never easy and the temptation to cling to the past is very strong, but God calls Samuel to recognize His hand in the matter of Saul's rejection and to move forward in God's work, not to live in the past.

"And Samuel said, How can I go? If Saul hear it, he will kill me..." (v. 2). Samuel's hesitancy is surprising from one who was so previously courageous. He was, however, a man of like passions with us.

The rapid decay of Saul's character was apparent to Samuel. No doubt, he knew that Saul, in his present frame of mind, was capable of virtually anything, even the assassination of God's prophet. To publicly anoint a new king while another king was presently sitting on the throne was extremely risky. What if Saul heard?

But God, who *"knoweth our frame and remembereth that we are but dust"* does not rebuke His servant. He deals with him in condescending mercy, reassuring him *"I will show thee what thou shalt do."* So *"Samuel did that which the Lord spake"* (v. 4).

Yes, God frequently calls upon His servants to perform potentially hazardous tasks, but His true servants will obey Him implicitly and completely (not like Saul), even in spite of their fears, trusting in the God of providence for protection.

God's Choice (vs. 6-13)

Jesse and his sons had been specially invited to Samuel's sacrifice. During this holy service, Samuel looked on Eliab, the oldest son, and said, *"Surely the Lord's anointed is before him"* (v.6). But the Lord had not chosen him. Then one by one, Jesse paraded his sons before Samuel—Abinadab, Shammah, and the rest—until all seven had passed before the prophet's gaze, but God had not chosen them.

Beginning to wonder, no doubt, why he had been sent to Jesse's house, Samuel inquired, *"Are here all thy children?"* Jesse replied, *"There remaineth yet the youngest, and behold, he keepeth the sheep"* (v. 11). That Jesse had not even considered David as a potential candidate is evident by the fact that he had not even been permitted to attend the sacred service. When he was summoned, the Lord spoke to Samuel and said, *"Arise, anoint him, for this is he"* (v. 12).

Why didn't the Lord simply say in the first place, "Go anoint David"? Why this elaborate ceremony of suspense'? He intended to teach that in the unfolding of His providence, His ways are frequently imperceptible and mysterious to natural reasoning: *"The Lord seeth not as man seeth; for man looketh on the outward appearance, but the Lord looketh on the heart"* (v. 7). This is a very important lesson to learn in every believer's life.

"And the Spirit of the Lord came upon David from that day forward" (v. 13). This was the beginning of a new stage in David's life, marked by a supernatural endowment from God for ministry.

That David went immediately back to the fields as a shepherd, however, is clear (v. 19). Could it have been during the subsequent days and weeks, in the verdant meadows of Bethlehem's hills and under the canopy of God's heaven, that David, under the Holy Spirit's sacred influence, composed the psalms celebrating the grandeur of God's Creation, like Psalm 8, 19, and 104?

Saul's Dementia (vs. 14-15)

In contrast to the Spirit of the Lord resting upon David, verse fourteen indicates His departure from Saul: *"But the Spirit of the Lord departed from Saul, and an evil spirit from the Lord troubled [lit. terrified] him."* Saul, suddenly, began to exhibit bouts of temporary insanity.

"His state of mind," writes Krummacher, "makes us scarcely able to recognize the man once so cheerful and vigorous in action. His eye appears fixed, his lips are violently compressed, and his whole countenance speaks of a deep, bitter animosity and gloom...Who would not pity this unhappy man?"[1]

A cold and black darkness now set in upon his brow. A dense fog of seething inner anger and agitation now settled heavily upon his heart. What is it that torments this man who has so many outward reasons for happiness and contentment? He has been abandoned by God and given over to "an evil spirit from the Lord."

Matthew Henry writes, "They that drive the good Spirit away from them, do of course become a prey to the evil spirit. If God and His grace do not rule us, sin and Satan will have possession of us."

How frightening a prospect to be "given over to a reprobate mind!" What a tragedy when "the glory of God departs" and "Ichabod" is written over a person's life! Satan and his evil angels are all too ready to fill the vacuum that has been left when God in his displeasure withdraws His providential influence and restraints from one who has presumptuously sinned against Him.

Interestingly, Scripture frequently (as in Saul's case) links the most bizarre behavior to unrepented sin in an individual's life. Consider the cases of Nebuchadnezzar's insanity in Daniel 4, and the wild man of Gadara in Mark

5. Could this not be the explanation in some cases (certainly, not in every case) where people have been diagnosed with insanity and dementia today? Is it not possible that the problem in some cases is not physical or organic at all, but spiritual? When the Lord because of persistent sin withdraws His blessing and influence from a person's life, how great is the darkness that floods the mind!

Music's Power (vs. 16-23)

Is there any help for a person in Saul's mental state? That question begged an answer in the mind's of Saul's courtiers as they observed the king's demonic moods which lay like a dark shadow over the whole palace.

They had long observed the change in his countenance and finally, one had the courage to propose a solution: *"Let our lord now command thy servants...to seek out a man who is a cunning player on a harp: and when the evil spirit from God is upon thee, he shall play with his hand, and thou shalt be well"* (v. 16).

Music is a powerful medium. The 18th century English dramatist William Congreve wrote, "Music has charms to soothe a savage breast, to soften rocks, or bend a knotted oak." He's correct. The right kind of melody with a masterful harmony and metrical rhythm can bring a pleasure to the mind and calmness to the emotions that is simply amazing. By the same token, the dissonance of a vulgar kind of music may cater to a person's basest instincts, altering moods for the worse. Yes, music is a powerful medium.

Interestingly, of all the conceivable musicians that might have been selected, David was the chosen harpist. They summoned to the royal palace with the instruction to bring his harp. Surely, his mind was in a whirl. "What might this mean?" he must have wondered. To those living in the middle of these circumstances, the events appear to be very random and circumstantial. But to those of us who have the benefit of knowing the larger significance of the story, the choice of David to be Saul's harpist is clearly providential. God is paving the way for David to assume the throne.

As David played with skillful hand, *"Saul was refreshed and was well, and the evil spirit departed from him"* (v. 23).

Notice that David's harp music had the capacity to drive the evil spirit away, but not to bring God's Spirit back. Music's power is merely temporary. It provides a kind of therapy, but it doesn't provide a cure for spiritual maladies. It treats the symptom, but cannot help the disease. Only repentance before God would cure Saul's soul disease.

God's Providence

Remarkably, God brought the king-elect from the sheepfold into the King's royal palace and immediate presence. No one, not even Saul, was conscious of how God was working behind the scenes to pave the way for David to assume the throne.

What providence that the future king was afforded an opportunity to observe first-hand the ways of the royal palace and receive the necessary training for his future role! That Saul "loved David greatly" (v.21) and that David "found favor in his sight" (v. 22) is a further testimony to the wise providence of God.

"The king's heart is in the hand of the Lord; He turneth it whithersoever He will as rivers of water" (Pro. 21:1). God was directing David's ascent to the throne, without any need

for David to force the door open or promote himself. Oh, the depth of the riches of the wisdom and knowledge of God!

---

[1] Krummacher, p. 31

Chapter 3
God's Giant, Israel's Champion
1 Samuel 17

First Samuel 17 might be titled "David's Great Confidence in the Lord." It records one of the most celebrated moments in Israel's history and one of the most significant displays of faith and courage in human history.

It is another illustration of the principle, *"God seeth not as man seeth, for man looketh on the outward appearance, but God looketh on the heart."* Goliath was physically superior to David, but David's strength was in the Lord his God. Through God David did valiantly and through the shepherd boy David, God tread down his enemies (Ps. 60:12). The true giant in this narrative was David, a giant in faith.

A Giant Challenge

The narrative begins by announcing a new conflict in the form of a military campaign by the Philistines, Israel's archenemy. As the two armies faced each other across the valley of Elah, the champion of the Philistines, an imposing figure standing 9½ feet tall, issued a defiant challenge: *"Give me a man, that we may fight together"* (vs. 9-10).

Champion warfare, in which two opposing armies settled a conflict by a dual between their respective representatives, was commonplace in oriental cultures. If the champion won, the entire army participated in the victory.[1]

Giant Cowardice

Goliath continued taunting the army of Israel every morning and evening for forty days. Twice a day, every soldier in Saul's army was forced to contemplate his own cowardice and fear. The pressure on them, however, could not possibly compare with the pressure on King Saul.

As the king of Israel, not to mention the most impressive physical specimen of the Hebrew army, Saul must have felt every eye upon him. If anyone might be expected to answer the challenge, it was Saul. But like the rest of his soldiers, Saul hid from the task in fear and intimidation. The army of Israel had every reason to trust in the arm of the Almighty God, but they trembled in fear before the arm of flesh because their king was fainthearted.

Giant Contempt

During this period of relentless humiliation from the giant of Gath, Jesse commissioned his youngest son, relieved of his duties in the palace while the "men" were away at war, to carry provisions to his brothers and inquire of their welfare. Just then, as David arrived on the scene, the threatening Philistine emerged from his tent to mock the Israelite soldiers.

David, aghast at his insolence, could not believe his ears. Neither could he believe his eyes, for the men of Israel *"fled from him and were sore afraid"* (v. 24).

"Who is this uncircumcised Philistine," he wondered aloud, *"that he should defy the armies of the living God?"* (v. 26). Remarkably, that is the first mention of "God" in the entire narrative. Evidently everyone else had forgotten about God. Every soldier had failed to interpret the circumstances before him in spiritual terms. Not David.

When David's brother Eliab overheard his little brother, he scolded him: *"Why camest thou down hither? And with whom hast thou left those few sheep in the wilderness? I know thy pride, and the naughtiness of thine heart; for thou art come down that thou mightest see the battle"* (v. 28). Eliab is embarrassed by his kid brother. His words mean, "You're just a kid. You have no business here. Go home to your sheep. Leave this business to the men and stop showing out." David responded, *"Is there not a cause?"*

Is there not a cause? David had an insight into this entire episode that no one else possessed. He saw Goliath's challenge as a spiritual issue—a "cause" for the glory and integrity of God's name. He was not, as Eliab suggested, driven by his own ego, but by the deep conviction that the glory of God was at stake. The name of God was being desecrated by an infidel. This was no mere "issue"—this was a "cause" that demanded action, for the glory of God! He could not conceal his holy zeal. God had called him, a mere stripling, to stop the mouth of this gainsayer.

Giant Confidence

Before long, the shepherd-boy is the talk of the camp. When tidings came to Saul that a young lad was challenging the insolence of the giant, David was summoned. With great tact lest he should accuse the king, David said, *"Let no man's heart fail because of him; thy servant will go and fight with this Philistine"* (v. 32).

Saul's "knee-jerk" response is predictable: *"Thou are not able...for thou art but a youth, and he a man of war from his youth"* (v. 33). His words mean, "You are out of your league, young man. He has you outsized and out-experienced."

David had no chance. Sheer common sense forbade Saul to allow it. It would be cruel to send this boy into battle, not to mention embarrassing. The stakes, furthermore, were too high. If he failed the entire nation would become slaves to the Philistines. A battle of these proportions demanded the best that Israel had to offer.

David, however, was undaunted. *"Thy servant slew both the lion and the bear. . . The Lord that delivered me out of the paw of the lion and out of the paw of the bear, he will deliver me out of the hand of this Philistine"* (vs. 36-37). His confidence in God made him courageous and convinced Saul that through the strength of the Lord, victory was indeed possible. *"Go, and the Lord be with thee,"* replied Saul.

A Giant Conquest

David then chose five smooth stones and with sling in hand, approached the moment of crisis. When Goliath saw the young boy, however, he was livid: *"Am I a dog,"* he said with curled lip, *"that you come at me with sticks?"* And he cursed David by his gods.

But with uncommon valor and unshaken faith, David replied, *"I come to thee in the name of the Lord of hosts. ..This day the Lord will deliver thee into mine hand. . .that all the earth may know that there is a God in Israel...for the battle is the Lords"* (vs. 45-47).

Taking a stone from the shepherd's bag, David whirled his sling. The stone flew like a lead ball from the bore of a muzzleloader and found its target, sinking into the giant's forehead. Goliath fell face down, dead cold. *"So David prevailed over the Philistine with a sling and with a stone"* (v. 50).

Giant Faith in a Giant God

This remarkable historical account is not merely a story about a young man's courage. It's not a story about David at all, but about David's God.

No "giant" intimidates our sovereign God. No problem is too gigantic for Him. Those who "know their God," like David, "will be strong and do exploits" (Dan. 11:32). With a clear sight of the One who displays His phenomenal strength in man's weakness to bring to nothing the things that are mighty, even the faintest heart will be courageous and bold as a lion.

It has been said that courage is the product of both conviction and conscience. David had both. His conviction that the glory of God's name was at stake, coupled with a conscience that would not allow him to remain idle before this outrage compelled him to enter the arena of personal sacrifice.

I would add to those two characteristics a third: confidence in God. Courage results when people of conviction and conscience meet a threatening challenge with complete confidence in the Lord. To such courageous champions of faith, God promises to show Himself strong.

---

[1] The epitome of the concept of "champion warfare" is the substitutionary sacrifice of the Lord Jesus Christ in the stead of his elect people. Christ fought the battle singlehandedly and "by himself purged us from our sins" (Heb. 1:3). This concept, then, is at the heart of the Christian gospel (cf. Rom. 5:18ff; 2 Cor. 5:21; 1 Pet. 3:18).

Chapter 4
Passions in the Palace
1 Samuel 18

"Love is strong as death and jealousy is cruel as the grave" (S.S. 8:6). These words from David's son Solomon are a fitting introduction to 1 Samuel 18.

The narrative of this remarkable chapter is a composite of both holy and unholy passions. Jonathan's loyal love and David's respectful behavior shine brilliantly as models of godliness, but Saul's perverse jealousy and paranoia give evidence to the depths of human depravity.

A.W. Pink suggested that an appropriate title for 1 Samuel 18 might be "The Price of Popularity." When someone is suddenly catapulted to fame, notoriety, and success, he becomes a target of jealousy and envy. Ecclesiastes 4:4 says, *"I considered...every right work, that for this a man is envied of his neighbor."* That's the price David paid for his exploits on the field of battle.

But such trials may be useful to God's servants, for they tend to counter the tendency to pride that success provides. In the palace of Saul, David faced a new season of danger a world removed from the quiet hillsides of Bethlehem that he had known previously in his life.

A Noble Friend (vs. 1-4)

Prior to the onslaught of this new trial, God mercifully gave the young hero a very special blessing, i.e. the friendship of Jonathan. Something about David's humble and virtuous disposition drew like cords upon Jonathan's heart.

How remarkable when one considers that Jonathan was the "heir apparent" to the throne! Yet Jonathan was not the least bit envious. He did not view David as a rival, for God had given David favor in the eyes of Jonathan. The covenant of friendship love between David and Jonathan, as the subsequent narrative proves, was "strong as death."

God frequently demonstrates His merciful providence in the lives of His people by giving them companions to deal with them kindly in times of great trial and crisis. Just as He comforted Paul by the coming of Titus (2 Cor. 7:6), He encouraged David by the gift of Jonathan's fellowship.

A Noble Servant (vs. 5, 14-16, 30)

Four times in the narrative we read *"and David behaved himself wisely."* Though his circumstances had changed, his character remained the same. The Hebrew word *sakal*, translated "wisely," implies judicious conduct. It is used in reference to self-control in Proverbs 10:19: *"In the multitude of words there wanteth not sin: but he who restrains his lips is wise [sakal]."*

In all his attitudes and actions, David demonstrated a servant's spirit toward Saul. Again, God honored him by giving him favor in the eyes of all the soldiers and people of Israel.

Popularity tends to go to a person's head. Saul's own history is an object lesson of that principle. When one's name becomes a household word—when everybody loves you—it's easy to lose perspective. David, however, did not forget who he was (vs. 18, 23). Who can refrain from admiring this noble young man?

An Ignoble King (vs. 6-29)

While Jonathan displays true selflessness and David true self-control, Saul begins to view David with suspicion (v. 9). The "green eyed monster" of jealousy rose from the depths of Saul's depraved heart.

The narrative records four attempts Saul made on David's life. Twice he sought to pin David to the wall with his javelin (v. 11). He positioned David at the head of a thousand men in battle against the Philistines in the hope that he would be slain (v. 17). Finally he required David to bring as Michal's dowry one hundred Philistine foreskins, a task that would expose him to grave danger (v. 25). In every case, however, David was unscathed. God was protecting His faithful servant.

Why was Saul so insanely jealous? Verse twelve answers, *"because the Lord was with him* [that is, David], *and was departed from Saul."* Aware of his own rapid inward disintegration, fear gripped his imagination and envy boiled within his soul.

Deep down, he knew he was witnessing his own demise as Israel's king, but instead of halting the downward slide by repenting of his sins, Saul attempted to destroy the one he considered to be his competitor. Jealous people always react in a rage of unjust hatred toward those whose lives are marked by God's singular blessing.

Saul's problem, you see, wasn't with David. It was with God. Like Cain before him, if he had "done well [i.e. in obedience to God]" he would have been accepted, but now sin was at the door.

Application

Few emotions are as destructive as envy, both to the one who in whom the attitude resides and the one toward whom the passion is directed. Concerning the perpetrator, jealousy affects one's health and happiness: *"A sound heart is the life of the flesh, but envy is as rottenness in the bones"* (Pro. 14:30). Concerning the victim, Proverbs 27:4 says, *"Wrath is cruel, and anger is outrageous: but who is able to stand before envy?"*

Envy destroys (cf. Job 5:2) because it drives a person to ever deepening levels of madness and hostility toward another. It is a violation of the second great commandment, *"Thou shalt love thy neighbor as thyself"* and is never, under any circumstances, befitting to a Christian (1 Pet. 2:1; 1 Cor. 13:4; Jas. 5:9).

But even more than the fact that it is a violation of the second great commandment, jealousy is at its root a sin against God for it demonstrates disapproval against His benevolent providence. When a person deems it unfair that God would allow someone else to enjoy a certain success or have a certain possession, he is murmuring against the dispensations of Divine providence. He has forgotten that God has the right to do as He pleases, that He is not obligated to us in any way, and that anything short of eternal judgment is a mercy from His hand.

How should a Christian respond when he feels the slightest twinge of jealousy arise in his heart? *First, he should remember his position as a servant.* We are not called to build personal empires to our own glory, but to serve Jesus Christ. We must never lose sight of the fact that our current position or station in life is a privilege, not a personal right.

Second, he must work on improving his own relationship with God instead of trying to destroy the perceived rival. The jealous person is usually discontent with his own circumstances and deeply afraid that others will discover the spiritual void in his life. The only solution to the dilemma is to resolve the problem of the spiritual void.

Finally, he must bow in submission to the fact that God is sovereign. He has the right to bless others as He pleases and "our eye should never be evil because He is good." Because it is so damaging to men and dishonoring to God, jealousy must never be allowed to gain a foothold in the believer's thoughts or attitudes.

It was during this experience that David penned Psalm 27: *"The Lord is my light and my salvation; whom shall I fear? The Lord is the strength of my life; of whom shall I be afraid."* Faced with Saul's passionate madness, David found strength in Jonathan's friendship. It was his confidence in God, his "light, salvation, and the strength of his life," that equipped him with the resources to carry on in the midst of these days of turmoil, behaving himself wisely.

Chapter 5
The Swallow Seeking a Nest
1 Samuel 19

From the quiet pastoral scenes of the sheep country to the notoriety and acclaim of a celebrity, David is now thrust into the hazardous life of a fugitive and exile. First Samuel 19-20 records a sequence of events in which David is driven from every form of security until, at last, he has no asylum or sanctuary but the Lord.

Saul, no longer able to hide his jealousy, publicizes his intention to slay David. For the next several years, he will literally hunt David like a partridge. And like a bird searching for a safe place to lay her eggs, David will flee from one potential sanctuary to another seeking refuge from the demented monarch.

Ultimately, the banished warrior will find permanent security from both physical danger and personal despair in the truth of the providence of God: *"The sparrow hath found a house, and the swallow a nest for herself, where she may lay her young, even thine altars, O Lord of Hosts, my King, and my God"* (Ps. 84:3; Cf. Ps. 11:1-4).

The Dark Providence of God

In the unfolding narrative of these chapters, one dominant theme surfaces. The entire drama is an illustration of what old writers called "The Dark Providence of God."

Why did they refer to God's providence by the adjective "dark"? Because the Lord's intervention in the lives of His people is frequently mysterious and imperceptible, at least at the first. Proverbs 20:24 says, *"Man's goings are of the Lord; how can a man then understand his own way?."*

Sometimes, in fact, it appears that He has set His own hand against us by virtue of the difficulties we encounter, or has totally withdrawn His aid and abandoned us to the enemy. In the end, however, it is apparent that the Lord had a "master plan" for the ultimate good of His servant and glory of His own name. Under this umbrella theme, several practical principles emerge from this narrative.

First, the difficult and thorny path of affliction may prove to be the way of sanctification. The whole of our training in godliness tends to the crucifying of the flesh. In His purpose to make His servants spiritually strong and totally dependent on Him, God removes from them every crutch and other source of security, weaning them more and more from earthly objects, until they seek their all in Him.

No doubt as David, partridge-like, is "flushed out" of first the palace and then his home, to a life of exile and flight, he might be tempted to think that God had abandoned him. Friedrich Krummacher asks, "A man according to God's own heart...but who that sees him now, hunted like a wild beast, would ever think that he was so highly accounted of by God?" But contrary to the apparent circumstances, God, in his "dark" providence, was indeed at work to further David's sanctification. "When the gold is in the crucible, the Refiner is near."

Secondly, God is in control even though the situation appears to be chaotic. Psalm 76:10 says, *"Surely the wrath of man shall praise thee: the remainder of wrath shalt thou restrain."* Though Saul was out of control, God was still exercising a restraining influence upon him. His anger was under God's control!

David, furthermore, was visibly protected by God. Through Jonathan's intercession (vs. 1-6), his escape from Saul's javelin (vs. 7-10), Michal's intervention to foil the conspiracy to slay him in his bed (vs. 11-17), and the spirit of prophecy that fell upon Saul and his messengers at Naioth (vs. 18-24), it is evident that God was frustrating Saul's wicked plot to slay David. *"The Lord bringeth the counsel of the heathen to naught: he maketh the devices of the people of none effect"* (Ps. 33:10).

Thirdly, in His merciful providence, God provides a momentary reprieve in the midst of our difficulties. the numerous attempts on his life, David fled to Ramah to see Samuel (v. 18). Obviously, he went to the godly prophet for encouragement, counsel, and asylum. He told him all that Saul had done to him. In a time of perplexity it is right to seek out the wisdom and comfort of those who are godly.

Samuel took David to Naioth where was "a school of the prophets." Surrounded by godly men of a kindred spirit, David's soul must have been wonderfully refreshed. The time with Samuel and the young prophets at Naioth was a providential oasis in the desert of his persecution.

Application

What was going on in the mind of David at this turbulent time in his life? Psalm 59, a product of David's heart (and pen) the night Saul's messengers surrounded his house, provides the answer.

It reveals that it was not the fear of death that concerned him the most, but a deep passion for the glory of God. In his moment of crisis David prayed, *"Deliver me from mine enemies, O my God: defend me from them that rise up against me"* (v. 1). David trusted completely in his God and found in Him a refuge of safety and asylum.

There is a message in this account for everyone who is persecuted without a cause. Few experiences in life are as painful as mistreatment. To be falsely accused or victimized by the sin and bitterness of another is unspeakably painful. David models, however, the kind of overcoming faith our Lord describes when he teaches his disciples to consider themselves "blessed" when they are persecuted for righteousness' sake (Mt. 5:10-11).

There is also a message here for those who are perplexed by their circumstances. Like Paul, David was no doubt perplexed, but he was not in despair (2 Cor. 4:7). He continued to trust his sovereign God even though he didn't necessarily understand what William Cowper called "a frowning Providence."

Finally, there is a message in this chapter for every pilgrim. When one is forced from the safety and security of the ordinary into the uncertainty and unfamiliarity of the unknown, God intends to emphasize by that experience the pilgrim nature of the Christian life and to remind his servant not to become too attached to this world. After all, there is no security in this world. The believer's only safety is in the Lord. So, "flee," my brother or sister, "flee as a bird to your mountain."

> God moves in a mysterious way
> His wonders to perform;
> He plants His footsteps in the sea,
> And rides upon the storm.
>
> Deep in unfathomable mines
> Of never-failing skill
> He treasures up His bright designs,

And works His sovereign will.

Ye fearful saints, fresh courage take,
The clouds ye so much dread
Are big with mercy, and shall break
In blessings on your head.

Judge not the Lord by feeble sense,
But trust Him for His grace;
Behind a frowning providence
He hides a smiling face.

His purposes will ripen fast,
Unfolding every hour;
The bud may have a bitter taste,
But sweet will be the flower.

Blind unbelief is sure to err,
And scan his work in vain;
God is His own interpreter,
And He will make it plain.

- William Cowper

Chapter 6
Covenant Loyalty
1 Samuel 20

The spotlight shifts now from David to Jonathan, the king's noble-hearted son. First Samuel 20 is one of the most striking examples of hallowed friendship in the Bible.

No other episode in Biblical history, except the cross, so encapsulates the words of Jesus: *"Greater love hath no man than this, that a man lay down his life for his friend."* Jonathan's self-denying love for the son of Jesse speaks to those of us who claim friendship with David's greater son, the Lord Jesus, as a model of loyalty that deserves to be emulated.

First Samuel 20 presents two powerful practical lessons: First, it teaches that **Pressure tends to weaken resolve and blur spiritual vision.** We must be especially careful in those seasons when the pressure is intense to continue to live by faith, and to resist the temptation to plot, scheme, and conspire.

David, unnerved by the pressure he faces, loses a clear focus on his God and begins to take matters into his own hands. As a result, for the first time in the sacred narrative of his life, he resorts to a kind of pragmatism. Like Abraham, fearing for his own safety, panicked before Pharaoh and said, "Sarai is my sister" (Gen. 12:11-20), David told a "little white lie" to justify his absence at Saul's feast (1 Sam. 20:5-6). Had not the Lord proved his ability to deliver David thus far? Was it not clear that God intended to protect His anointed from Saul?

Secondly, this chapter teaches that **Loyalty to God inevitably places us in situations where a sacrifice must be made, sometimes at great personal cost.** Jonathan, torn between respect for and obedience to his father yet affection and admiration for David, is faced with a situation in which he is forced to make a choice between the two. Will he be loyal to his father the king by joining him in the plot to slay David, or will he be loyal to the one whom God had chosen to one day occupy the throne not only in the place of his father, but at the loss of his own crown rights?

The tension in Jonathan's heart must have been incredible. Loyalty to David meant perceived disloyalty to and betrayal of his own father. Loyalty to Saul meant participation, either directly or indirectly, in treachery and sin.

The moral dilemma he faces is great. Shall he participate in his father's conspiracy against an innocent man out of a sense of obligation to his own flesh and blood, or shall he stand for righteousness and justice at the risk of what Saul would perceive as a conspiracy against himself?

When the fact that Jonathan's own future as the king of Israel was jeopardized by David's existence is added to the equation, the issue is complicated even further. Though he must have struggled inwardly over the tension between loyalty to his father and loyalty to his friend, Jonathan chose to aid and abet the son of Jesse, "to," in Saul's words, "his own confusion" (v. 30), but to, no doubt, the peace of his own unoffended conscience. He nobly sacrificed his own interests and made a covenant promise to his godly friend.

What influenced his choice? The conviction that his father was behaving disobediently to God. Jonathan's loyalty to David arose first and foremost from his sense of loyalty to God.

Because of man's inherent depravity, people tend to use and exploit other people to their own advantage. Jonathan, however, is a refreshing exception to that rule.

Facing tremendous pressure to put allegiance to "family" over faithfulness to the law of God, Jonathan opted to please the Lord at the cost of great personal sacrifice, and he did it joyfully, for he *"loved David as he loved his own soul."* To New Testament saints whose loyalty to the Lord Jesus Christ, the Super David, is frequently tested in similar ways, even to the point of choosing between faithfulness to Him and allegiance to one's family, Jonathan's covenant loyalty and self-sacrificing love provide a model worth duplicating. Whose side are you on?

Chapter 7
David Stumbles
1 Samuel 21

Martin Luther said, "To have God always before the eyes makes a lively spirit and an undismayed heart, which is joyful and willing to bear patiently wherever misfortune, the cross, and suffering need to be borne: such a faith is unconquerable." David's exploits heretofore have testified to the truth of those words.

Now, however, as an outlaw and a fugitive, David temporarily loses sight of God and stumbles in unbelief. Instead of doing the right thing in confident trust, the one whom neither beast nor giant could shake, now, under the pressure of persecution, sinks to the unprecedented depth of telling lies and practicing deceit. Learn from this brief episode in David's life that even the strongest saints can stumble through the weakness of the flesh, especially in a time when the Lord is eclipsed by the difficulties of the way.

The Circumstances

David's flight from Saul now takes him to Nob where Ahimelech the priest is ministering in the tabernacle. Startled by David's sudden (and probably unkempt) appearance, Ahimelech asked *"Why art thou alone?"*

David replied that he was on an urgent mission for the king and needed bread to sustain him on his journey. Though the only bread available in the tabernacle was the twelve loaves of shewbread that had just that morning been removed to make way for the new loaves, Ahimelech gave the holy bread to David, for works of necessity and of mercy were permitted on the Sabbath day (cf. Mt. 12:1-7).

By a lie, David had obtained his provisions. The end, however, does not justify the means.

Compounding his deception, David then asks Ahimelech for a weapon, stating pretentiously that his hasty departure prohibited him from bringing his own sword with him. The only weapon available was sword of Goliath, wrapped in an ephod. David said, "Give it to me, for there is none like it."

Isn't it strange that David was worried by the prospect of being unarmed? Krummacher states, "Once the shepherd's sling alone was necessary for our hero; now he asks for that sword which had not even availed him for whose giant hand it had been fabricated...Poor David!"

With consecrated bread and Goliath's sword in hand, David then fled for asylum to the Philistine city of Gath, Goliath's home-town, carrying Goliath's sword. One wonders whether David has not completely lost his sound judgment! Arthur Pink comments, "Common prudence might have taught him, that, if he sought the friendship of the Philistines, the sword of Goliath was not the most likely instrument to conciliate their favor."

Perhaps he imagined that enemy territory would be the only safe refuge from Saul, and that under the pretense of defection from Saul's army, the Philistines would receive him gladly. It didn't take long, however, for the citizens of Gath to recognize him.

According to the caption of Psalm 56, a Psalm composed on this occasion, the Philistine lords seized him prisoner and brought him before Achish the king. Waiting to be admitted before the king, David pretended to be insane, scribbling on the walls and drooling all over himself.

Is this the same courageous warrior who stood toe-to-toe with the enemy in the strength of the Lord God of hosts? Indeed, his tactic was successful and David was released, but he would look back on his behavior with sorrow.

The Consequences

Standing in the shadows of the tabernacle that day was Doeg the Edomite. Doeg was the chief of Saul's herdsmen. He also became Saul's informant of the transactions in Nob, and Saul's instrument in the assassination of Ahimelech and 85 priests, for aiding and abetting David.

First Samuel 22:6-23 records the grisly massacre. Though Saul and Doeg are primarily culpable for this treacherous slaughter, David recognizes that it was his deception that put the priest in a position of danger. To Abiathar, the sole survivor of the priestly family, David sorrowfully admits, *"I have occasioned the death of all the persons of thy father's house"* (22:22).

If he had but trusted God's providence, this catastrophe surely could have been avoided. Every little sin, however apparently harmless, may indeed reap great and sad consequences (Hos. 8:8).

The Cause

What could possibly account for David's strange behavior? Fear. David fled "for fear of Saul" (v. 10) and pretended to be insane because he was "sore afraid of Achish king of Gath" (v. 12). The shepherd boy who stood fearlessly before Goliath is now so overpowered by fear that he resorts to lies and tricks in an attempt at self-preservation.

But why would fear suddenly seize his heart now, after so many heroic and courageous exploits in the recent past? Somewhere in David's thoughts, he assumed that he was outside the scope of God's providence. Perhaps the pressure of adversity finally got to him. Maybe he concluded that his circumstances contradicted God's promise that he would be king. Exactly how it happened is not clear, but David lost touch with the Lord. When he ceased to fear God, he began to fear everything else.

Psalm 34 describes David's feelings in the aftermath of deliverance from king Achish of Gath. Its tranquil tone suggests it was written as David reflected in gratitude on the experience. It is in this Psalm that David recognizes that his greatest threat is not Saul, or the Philistines, but his own "fears" which can so easily blind him to the reality of God's promise: *"I sought the Lord, and he heard me, and delivered me from all my fears...This poor man cried, and the Lord heard him, and saved him out of all his troubles..."* (vs. 4,6).

The lesson David learned from this episode of momentary weakness would not soon be lost: *"Come, ye children, hearken unto me: I will teach you the fear of the Lord...Keep thy tongue from evil and thy lips from speaking guile...The eyes of the Lord are upon the righteous, and his ears are open to their cry...* (vs. 11-15). Maintaining focus on God, in other words, fosters faith and forbids the fear that leads to sin. That is a lesson every believer should remember.

Chapter 8
Misery's Company
1 Samuel 22:1-5; 2 Samuel 23:8-39
(cf. 1 Chr. 11:10 - 12:1-40)

In 1 Samuel 22, David takes refuge in the cave of Adullam, a "hold" in the wilderness. It is at this point in David's flight from Saul that something very surprising occurs. In an unexpected turn of events, four hundred disgruntled Israelites open the floodgates to what will become nothing less than a massive exodus from Saul's kingdom to ally themselves with David.

The initial group of defectors included David's father and brothers and four hundred social misfits. This, however, was only the beginning of David's personal army.

Commenting on this episode years later, the Chronicler informs, *"At that time day by day there came to David to help him, until it was a great host, like the host of God"* (1 Chr. 12:22). To what should we attribute this spontaneous gesture of support for David? Why did these men suddenly take their allegiance from Saul and give it to David?

Nothing short of Divine providence explains this extraordinary shift in momentum: *"And these...came to David to Hebron, to turn the kingdom of Saul to him, according to the word of the Lord"* (1 Chr. 12:23).

Misery

Psalm 142 was composed by David as he hid from Saul in the cave. Never had he been at such a low ebb. Listen to the lonely fugitive as he pours out his complaint before the Lord: *"I looked on my right hand, and beheld, but there was no man that would know me: refuge failed me; no man cared for my soul"* (v. 4).

Next, note his heart-cry: *"I cried unto Thee, O Lord: I said, Thou art my refuge and my portion...Attend unto my cry; for I am brought very low: deliver me from my persecutors; for they are stronger than I. Bring my soul out of prison that I may praise Thy name"* (vs. 5-7a).

Finally, observe his certainty of deliverance: *"The righteous shall compass me about; for thou shalt deal bountifully with me"* (v. 7).

Mercy

Krummacher comments, "This heart-cry from the lonely cave had found its way to the heart of the Almighty...Before even David is aware of it, 'the righteous' assemble themselves together unto him."

That this company of mercenaries voluntarily joined themselves to the lonely fugitive is a singular testimony to the fact that God answers the prayers of the righteous. How merciful is our God to give His faithful servants fellow 'outcasts' with whom they may share their mutual woes, comforting each other with the comfort that they themselves have received from the Lord (2 Cor. 1:3)!

Motives

Driven by their extremity, these four hundred men joined forces with David. The whole country groaned under the burden of Saul's disobedience. These men especially were pressed by exorbitant taxation and heavy debt. Perhaps they saw in David one who could empathize with them in their abject need.

He was also, no doubt, the man of their hopes. The sense that He was God's anointed king intensified in their hearts. Driven by their own need and yet by their conviction that God's hand was upon the son of Jesse, this makeshift army assembled under the banner of God's king-elect, and "he became a captain over them."

These men are not mere rebels who refused to pay their debts. They are not social malcontents who saw an opportunity to run away from responsibility. Psalm 142:7 calls them "the righteous."

Indeed, some of these men became David's bravest and most loyal subjects. From this assorted group of outcasts rose David's "mighty men of valor" (Cf. 2 Sam. 23:8-39). Driven by their own destitute condition and by a growing conviction that David was righteous in the eyes of God, they risked life and limb to stand beside one who was despised and rejected of men.

So, the followers of Jesus Christ must first come to the end of themselves before they will flee for refuge to the Man of their hopes. Sick of sin, oppressed by the devil, and dissatisfied with the world, they are driven by their own deep need to their David.

Yes, they are willing to be contemptible in the eyes of the world, for they have nowhere else to go. He has the words of eternal life (Jno. 6:68). So, Moses-like, they choose rather to suffer affliction with the people of God than to enjoy the pleasures of sin for a season.

Out of their "shameful failure and loss," they ally themselves to One who is despised and rejected of men, and he gives rest to their souls (Mt. 11:28). They gladly go forth unto Him without the camp, bearing His reproach, for He is "the Captain of their salvation," the brightest "Star" on the distant horizon.

Then they commit themselves to a lifetime of service and submission to Him. He is their leader and they His loyal subjects. They will fight His battles and show themselves valiant for their David, for He received them gladly when they were hopelessly bankrupt, wretched, and weak. Though they have lost their lives in Saul's kingdom, they have found abundant life and fulfillment in David's.

An alliance with the Lord Jesus Christ will require this same kind of choice, i.e. to deliberately renounce the past life and to ally ourselves to King Jesus, but sensible sinners who are weary and heavy laden have no other place to flee. So, "come ye sinners, poor and needy, weak and wounded, sick and sore; Jesus ready stands to help you, full of pity, love, and power."

Chapter 9
God, Our Shield and Defender
1 Samuel 23

After the momentary lapse in which he lost sight of the Lord (1 Sam. 21), David now regains his moment-by-moment trust in his God. Chapter 23 describes the circumstances in which God intervened to deliver David from Saul during his wilderness wanderings.

The narrative takes us first to Keilah (23:1-13), then to the wilderness of Ziph (23:14-23), then to the wilderness of Maon (23:24-29). Though David was betrayed by both the men of Keilah and the Ziphites (men from his own tribe of Judah), he was never abandoned by God, his Shield and Defender. It was during these wilderness wanderings that David wrote Psalm 27, 42, 54 and 63.

God Directs His Servants

With his newly assembled army of 400 men, David sets out on his first military campaign. News reaches him that Keilah has been invaded by the Philistines, so David "inquired of the Lord" whether to go to Keilah. Twice he sought God's guidance, and twice God answered him, *"Go and save Keilah, for I will deliver the Philistines into thy hand."*

Nobly, David forgets his personal difficulties for the moment to fight the battles of the Lord against Israel's traditional nemesis, Philistia. Though his men were hesitant to leave the fortification at Adullam, David led his men forward, according to the promise of the Lord, and God gave them the victory.

The promise and reality of Divine guidance is a dominant theme in the Psalter (Ps. 5:8; Ps. 23:3; Ps. 25:5; Ps. 27:11; Ps. 31:2-3, Ps. 32:8). The individual who lives by faith should always seek God's will instead of the "counsel of the ungodly" (Ps. 1:1).

"But," someone questions, "how does God communicate vocational guidance to His children?" In ancient times, he revealed his will through dreams, visions, and direct audible messages. Even in the New Testament, God directed Peter to Cornelius, Philip to the Ethiopian eunuch, and Paul to Macedonia by means of a vision.

He may, indeed, use such means, but I suspect that communicating His will via dreams and visions is not the general rule for determining the guidance of God. Although these methods of receiving Divine direction are exceptional instead of normal, however, they do suggest that God is not handcuffed in His ability to make His will known to His servants.

What, then, is God's regular method of communicating guidance? According to Colossians 1:9, God's will is discovered primarily through God's word.

Scripture guides us by giving certain general principles to follow in various situations. God will never direct someone to act contrary to His word. That's the first principle regarding guidance.

In those cases when God's word does not give specific vocational direction, God has promised to make His mind known in answer to prayer. The church at Antioch received confirmation through prayer that God had selected Paul and Barnabas for a certain work (Acts 13:2). How are we to understand this consensus of mind? We are to understand that the church reached agreement on what to do in terms of a growing inward conviction that God was in the matter.

Inner convictions, however, are not always reliable. Because of the principle expressed in Jeremiah 17:9, i.e. "The heart is deceitful...and desperately wicked: who can know it?" then self-distrust is always appropriate.

Two common pitfalls must be avoided when we speak of this inner prompting and inclination: (l) Fanaticism - The inner voice may not be the Holy Spirit; hence, perceived direction from God should be exposed to the checks and balances of godly and spiritually-minded people in the church (Pro. 11:14; 12:15; 13:10; 15:22); (2) Impatience - Usually, it is God's way to delay His answer so that providentially, more and more doors are shut, leaving only one open. By that means, He works to crystallize the sense in the heart that He has answered prayer (Is. 30:18). The spirit of impatience that runs ahead of the providential unfolding of circumstances only complicates the problem and increases the potential of missing God's best in our lives (Ps. 27:14; Is. 50:10-11).

God Protects His Servants

From Keilah, David fled to a mountain in the wilderness Of Ziph. *"And Saul sought him every day, but God delivered him not into his hand"* (v.14).

The Ziphites, however, betrayed David's position and conspired with Saul to deliver him to the king's hand. At that moment when it appeared that Saul would overtake David, a messenger appeared announcing, *"The Philistines have invaded the land"* (v. 27). Faced with this more urgent national crisis, Saul postponed his pursuit of David and returned to defend the country against the Philistines.

All in all, the narrative demonstrates that the Lord's arm is not too short to deliver. His abilities to rescue His true servants from danger are not limited.

Is it any wonder that David would exclaim *"When the wicked, even mine enemies came upon me...they stumbled and fell. Though an host should encamp against me, my heart shall not fear... [for] the Lord is my light and my salvation"* (Ps. 27)?

Chapter 10
God Avenges His Servants
1 Samuel 24

The last verse of 1 Samuel 23 reads, *"And David went up from thence, and dwelt in the strongholds at En-gedi."* Upon receiving this news, Saul gathered an army of 3,000 men to pursue David in these rocky highlands. Here, however, David met one of his most severe tests: the temptation to take vengeance into his own hands.

Unwittingly, Saul made his way into the very cave in which David and his men were hiding, and fell asleep. David's soldiers were quick to encourage him to end the injustice: *"Behold the day of which the Lord said unto thee, Behold, I will deliver thine enemy into thine hand, that thou mayest do to him as it shall seem good unto thee."* (24:4).

What should he do? Could it be that God had indeed delivered Saul into David's hand? Should he put an end to the madness that had characterized his life for the past months, maybe years?

When one has been the victim of injustice and mistreatment, the temptation to retaliate, to repay in kind, to "get even" is indescribably powerful. Ask anyone who has lived through a divorce, or been cheated out of a promotion at work or robbed of money. There is nothing more "natural" than to want to hurt those who have hurt us by capitalizing on an opportunity to exploit them in a time of misery.

David felt the power of the temptation and rose to cut a swath from Saul's robe. No sooner had the fabric torn, however, but David's *"heart smote him"* (v. 5).

He knew he had overstepped a line — a line that separates between God's righteous nature and man's responsibility to do what is consistent with righteousness, regardless of the consequences. By stretching forth his hand to take vengeance, David was, in effect, "playing God."

Though most people would consider David's action justifiable in the light of the circumstances, David's conscience screamed "That was wrong!" Though many would even say that he acted honorably in cutting his skirt instead of his neck, the Holy Spirit convicted him that he had wandered precariously into territory that belonged to God alone.

He had momentarily forgotten his own admonition: *"Fret not thyself because of evil doers...Cease from anger, and forsake wrath: fret not thyself in any wise to do evil"* (Ps. 37:1, 8).

"Vengeance is mine; I will repay, saith the Lord." The taking of vengeance is God's exclusive domain, for He alone is righteous. Though others speak words that cut like knives into the heart, the Christian is never justified to repay insult for injury. Even the spirit of revenge that waits with abated breath to see one's perceived enemy stumble or that rejoices at another's misfortune is a violation of God's role as judge: *"Rejoice not when thy enemy falleth, lest the Lord see it and it displease him"* (Pro. 24:17-18; Pro. 17:5; Job 31:29).

People like us who inevitably encounter mistreatment from our fellow sinners need frequent reminders like Romans 12:19: *"Dearly beloved, avenge not yourselves...be not overcome of evil, but overcome evil with good."*

Are you afraid that justice will not be served if you do not take matters into your own hand? Dismiss the fear, for God promises to avenge his servants. He will stand up to plead for them and insure that the scales of justice are equalized, either in this world or at the resurrection of the just.

Moments later when Saul awoke and exited the cave, David called to him, revealing that he had repaid evil with good in sparing his life. *"Mine hand shall not be upon thee,"* he vowed, *"[but] the Lord judge between me and thee, and the Lord avenge me of thee. . .the Lord see, and plead my cause, and deliver me out of thine hand"* (vs. 12, 15).

Our responsibility is to always do the right thing, trusting God to avenge, that is to silence the accusers and to validate the integrity of his true servants.

At this revelation, Saul humbled himself and confessed David's righteousness. For the moment, he abandoned his campaign to exterminate 'the man after God's own heart.' And David sat down and wrote Psalm 57:

Psalm 57

To the chief Musician, Altaschith, Michtam of David, when he fled from Saul in the cave.

¹Be merciful unto me, O God, be merciful unto me:
for my soul trusteth in thee: yea, in the shadow of thy wings will I make my refuge, until these calamities be overpast.
²I will cry unto God most high;
unto God that performeth all things for me.
³He shall send from heaven, and save me from the reproach of him that would swallow me up. Selah.
God shall send forth his mercy and his truth.
⁴My soul is among lions: and I lie even among them that are set on fire, even the sons of men, whose teeth are spears and arrows, and their tongue a sharp sword.
⁵Be thou exalted, O God, above the heavens;
let thy glory be above all the earth.
⁶They have prepared a net for my steps;
my soul is bowed down: they have digged a pit before me, into the midst whereof they are fallen themselves. Selah.
⁷My heart is fixed, O God, my heart is fixed:
I will sing and give praise.

⁸Awake up, my glory; awake, psaltery and harp:
I myself will awake early.
⁹I will praise thee, O Lord, among the people:
I will sing unto thee among the nations.
¹⁰For thy mercy is great unto the heavens,
and thy truth unto the clouds.
¹¹Be thou exalted, O God, above the heavens:
let thy glory be above all the earth.

Chapter 11
Divine Restraint
1 Samuel 25

Have you ever attempted to do a kind deed, only to be repaid by ingratitude, even insult, from the one who benefited from your courtesy? The typical "knee-jerk" reaction to such base ingratitude is anger.

Who has not experienced outrage at the apparent injustice of ingratitude? Everyone at one point or another will feel the powerful surge of passion that reacts against a perceived wrong. It's impossible to live in a world of injustices without it.

Anger, however, is an extremely dangerous emotion. In its own right, anger is not sinful. It is, in fact, a God-given emotion. Rare is the person, however, who can "be angry and sin not."

Anger produces a kind of insanity in which passion conquers reason and makes a person do "foolish" and irrational things. Consider, for instance, how the Bible equates anger with foolishness: *"Be not hasty in thy spirit to be angry: for anger resteth in the bosom of fools"* (Ecc. 7:9); *"He that is soon angry dealeth foolishly..."* (Pro. 14:17; cf. Pro. 20:3). It's simply not very smart to lose one's temper.

First Samuel 25 records an episode in the life of David in which he almost did something very foolish. Had it not been for God's restraining providence, David's temper might have caused him to commit great folly in Israel.

As all Israel mourned the passing of Samuel, David fled to the wilderness of Paran. A very wealthy man named Nabal (meaning "foolish") was busy harvesting wool from his large herd of sheep. David sent a small delegation of his servants to Nabal with tidings of peace and a request for food. The ten servants related the fact of David's unsolicited kindness to Nabal's shearers, protecting them from the Philistines while they sheared.

Nabal's response, however, was insolent. *"Who is David?"* he asked contemptuously. *"He's probably a renegade, fleeing from his master."*

Nabal, whose name, again, means "foolish," was certainly living up to his name. This behavior wasn't very smart, by any definition of the term. Of course, Nabal knew who David was. The insinuation that David was a turncoat who had "broken away from his master" was more than David could handle. He was livid.

"Gird ye on every man his sword" said David. *"Surely in vain have I kept all that this fellow hath in the wilderness...and he hath requited me evil for good."*

So, David set out to exterminate every male of the family of Nabal. The man who had recently resisted the urge to take vengeance on king Saul is now overcome by the intolerable sense that he has been violated. He will stop at nothing until his wrath is satisfied.

Because of his temper, David risked becoming a "Nabal" himself. It is always a foolish thing to react to any situation in haste (Pro. 14:29; 19:11; 16:32). The wrath of man never works the righteousness of God (Jas. 1:20).

Had it not been for Divine restraint upon David's life, he would have stooped to the level of the man Nabal: *"Blessed be the Lord who...hath kept his servant from evil"* he later sighed (v. 39).

Our sovereign God "makes the wrath of man to praise him, and the remainder of wrath he restrains" (Ps. 76:10). In other words, even when a person loses self-control—even when a person is 'out-of-control'—the Lord is still in control of the situation, exercising a restraining providence and withholding his people from their sinful potential (Gen. 20:6; Ex. 34:23-24).

The petition *"Lead us not into temptation but deliver us from evil"* in the Model Prayer is a recognition that left to ourselves we are prone to fall into the grossest of sinful behaviors and attitudes; consequently, we request that God would restrain us from those natural proclivities (Mt. 6).

How did God deliver David from himself? He used Nabal's wife, Abigail.

Playing the role of intercessor, this courageous and virtuous woman reminded David of God's promise. By her "soft answer," she "turned away his wrath." Upon her return, she discovered that God had dealt with Nabal, who suffered what was apparently a stroke so that he died. After his death, Abigail became David's wife.

The next time you are tempted to nurse an injury, remember the words of Amy Carmichael: *"...If I feel bitterly toward those who condemn me, as it seems to me unjustly, forgetting that if they knew me as I know myself they would condemn me much more, then I know nothing of Calvary love."*

Surely David's violent reaction would give him pause to consider that he too had a "Nabal" dwelling inside his heart. In fact, the potential for the worst of sins is resident in every depraved heart. Except for the grace of God, we may all be a "Nabal."

Chapter 12
The Closing of a Chapter
1 Samuel 26

First Samuel 26 records the final meeting of Saul and David. Though they did not know it at the time, never again would either see the face of the other in this life.

It marks, then, the closing of a chapter in David's life, and provides us with several practical lessons for consideration. It is a sad scene, for it reveals how Saul's madness has driven from him every godly influence, beginning with Samuel, then Jonathan, Abiathar the priest, Gad the prophet, and now his own faithful son-in-law, David.

The Priority of a Clear Conscience

Upon returning from the wilderness of Ziph, the Ziphites again betrayed David's position to Saul. This news stirred afresh the poison in his heart and Saul launched a new campaign to slay David.

When Saul and his men pitched camp in the hill of Hachilah, however, *"a deep sleep from the Lord fell upon them."* David and Abishai moved with stealth into the very camp of the slumbering army. Saul lay sleeping with his spear stuck in the ground and Abner, his general and chief bodyguard, also slept near him.

Abishai whispered, *"God hath delivered thine enemy into thine hand...let me smite him."* For the second time, David is faced with an opportunity to rid himself of his insane persecutor. Arthur W. Pink asks, "Had their positions been reversed, would Saul hesitate to slay him? Why, then, should David allow sentiment to prevail? Moreover, did it not look as though God had arranged things to this very end?"

But again, in spite of the temptation, principle rules over passion. David replies, *"Destroy him not: for who can stretch forth his hand against the Lord's anointed and be guiltless?"*

His patience is truly remarkable. He is willing to wait for the Lord's perfect timing, submit to the providence of God, and trust his case to the God who judges righteously: *"As the Lord liveth, the Lord shall smite him; or his day shall come to die; or he shall descend into battle, and perish"* (v. 10). Sooner or later, God would correct the injustice, just as He had done with Nabal.

David's refusal to lift his hand against Saul to his own advantage demonstrates the importance of conducting oneself at all times and in all circumstances in a way so that one does not have to live with a guilty conscience. David wanted to live in such a way that he would have no occasion for regret.

A clear conscience "toward God and toward man" (Acts 24:16) is inexpressibly sweet. It makes the step nimble and the burden light (1 Jno. 3:21-22). An offended conscience, on the contrary, is unspeakably bitter: *"Heaviness in the heart of man maketh it stoop."* The individual who has learned, like David, the priority of a clear conscience must be diligent to behave by principle rather than passion, by faith rather than feeling.

The Nature of True Repentance

Instead of striking Saul, David took Saul's spear and canteen and escaped to the top of the hill. From there, he called out to Abner, scolding him for carelessly putting the king's life in jeopardy. The humorous way that David taunts Abner provides a momentary relief from the emotional tension of the story.

In effect David says, "Abner, you are fueling Saul's rage by suggestions that I am his enemy, but I spared his life while you left him exposed to danger; now, who is really the king's friend?"

At this point, Saul confessed, *"I have sinned...I will no more do thee harm...behold, I have played the fool and have erred exceedingly"* (v. 21). He then tenderly invited David to "return," or to draw nigh.

Was his repentance genuine? David didn't think so. Though David's words suggest that he harbored no feelings of bitterness toward Saul, yet wisdom demanded caution: *"Let one of the young men come over and fetch"* the spear, he replied. Saul's goodness was fickle, "like the morning cloud" (Hos. 6:4), and David had every reason to be suspicious. It was not long ago that Saul had made a similar admission of his guilt, only to return to his former insanity.

True repentance involves both godly sorrow and the abandonment of sinful behavior. Did Saul abandon his campaign to slay David after this episode? Yes. But was his sorrow genuine? Was he full of remorse because he had sinned against God? If so, how could he have sought the counsel of the witch of Endor just two chapters later?

Something about Saul's demeanor gave David pause to accept back into his confidence this man who had long pursued him. Instead, David committed the case to the Lord: *"The Lord render to every man his righteousness and his faithfulness"* (v. 23). *"So David went on his way, and Saul returned to his place."*

Learn from this that forgiveness of a wrong does not necessarily mean that you receive the serial offender back into your total trust. Forgiveness means that you refuse to retaliate or settle the score, turning the case over to the Lord in the event that He intends to measure out justice. Trust, however, must be earned by evidence that proves the repentance is genuine.

Chapter 13
David's Spiritual Vacuum
1 Samuel 27

J C. Ryle wrote, "The best of men are only men at their very best. Patriarchs, prophets, and apostles - martyrs, fathers, reformers, puritans - all, all are sinners, who need a Savior: holy, useful, honorable in their place, but sinners after all."

First Samuel 27 provides us with an example of that principle in the life of David. There is no more shameful and disgraceful experience during this period of David's life than what is recorded here.

The theme of the chapter is compromise and like Lot pitching his tent toward Sodom, and Peter warming himself by the enemy's fire, David's apparent desertion to the Philistines stands as one of the most vivid examples of compromise in the Bible.

Unbelief Leads to Compromise

Those "who know the plague of their own hearts" are not surprised to read the sobering words of verse one: *"And David said...I shall now perish one day by the hand of Saul..."*

Like Elijah sat under a juniper tree and requested to die after his victory at Mt. Carmel, David, in the aftermath of his latest triumph of faith lost sight of God and sunk into unbelief. He fled once more to Gath to take refuge among Israel's perennial enemy, the Philistines.

For the next sixteen months (v. 7), David lived in a state of compromise. It is remarkable that no Psalms were produced from David's pen during this period of his life. He was, in a very real sense, in a spiritual vacuum.

The Holy Spirit has said, *"Now the just shall live by faith; but if any man draw back, my soul shall have no pleasure in him"* (Heb. 10:38). Now, the reality was that Saul would no more pursue David (v. 4) and would, in short order, be slain in battle (1 Sam. 31). David had but to wait patiently on the Lord, but doubt and fear vexed his imagination. The weary fugitive thus "leaned upon his own understanding" (Pro. 3:5). He lived by sight and sense, not by faith. How many times have we allowed fear to drive us to imagine the worst and to grip our hearts with a panic of doubt and unbelief?

Not once in this chapter do we read that David prayed. His decision to flee to king Achish was strictly the product of carnal reasoning. When a person is out of touch with God, they can do some very irrational things. David was a Hebrew, but now he attempts to make the Philistines believe that he is one of them.

Frederich Krummacher says, "In order to recommend himself to the goodwill of his protector, [David] led him to believe that, as he had renounced allegiance to King Saul, so he had also laid aside the national hatred of his people against the heathen; and by doing this David already made himself guilty of a culpable abandonment of the truth."

Compromise Has its Consequences

David's compromise contains a number of practical lessons for believers who are tempted to make friends with the world. ***First, it gave occasion to the adversary to speak reproachfully***. In appearing to be a friend of the Philistines, David assumed the stance of a traitor to his country.

Achish *"believed David, saying 'He hath made his people Israel utterly to abhor him; therefore he shall be my servant forever"* (27:12). Oh, the disgrace and shame that David must have felt in his conscience to know that he was living a lie by appearing to be someone he was not!

Secondly, compromise put his companions and his family in danger. David's six hundred soldiers and his two wives were travelling with him (27:3). This excursion into the country of the enemy exposed them to needless danger. Surely, no man lives to himself or dies to himself. Compromise necessarily affects those around us.

Third, this one false step led to others, namely deception and dishonesty. To quiet his wounded conscience, he launched a military campaign against some of Israel's enemies, the Geshurites, Gergesites, and Amalekites, heathen tribes that had not been driven out by Joshua. But when he returned with the spoils of the battle, he led Achish to infer that he had been fighting with his own people (27:8-10). Lest his tactics should be discovered by a lone survivor, David covered his tracks by slaying every man and woman (v. 11).

Finally, it put him in the precarious position of having to take up arms against his own people. The ultimate test came when Achish revealed to David that he expected him to lead the Philistine army in a new battle against the Israelites (28:1-2).

Now he must take the sword against his own people under the banner of Israel's enemy. In compromise, he had sown the wind; now, he would reap the whirlwind. Indeed, what a tangled web we weave, when first we practice to deceive.

Chapter 14
The End of the Road for Saul
1 Samuel 28

King Saul reminds one of the proud emperor in Hans Christian Anderson's children's classic who paraded through the streets of the city in his invisible clothes until a little boy courageously shouted the obvious: "The emperor has no clothes." First Samuel 28 is the Biblical equivalent of that revelation. This is the end of the road for Saul, the final act in the life of a man who had been righteously abandoned by God.

His final act reveals the depths to which he had sunk, for nothing can scarce be as reprehensible as witchcraft. Driven by panic at a new Philistine invasion, Saul "inquired of the Lord" for guidance, but "the Lord answered him not" (28:6).

His appeal was driven by desperation, not repentance (see 1 Chr. 10:13). Totally abandoned by God, Saul did the unthinkable: he appealed to the witch of Endor.

God had expressly stated in the law *"The soul that setteth itself to go those that have familiar spirits, I will even set myself against that soul"* (Lev. 20:6). To fail to seek the Lord is a great sin; to seek him and not find him should spur one to self-examination and repentance; but to blatantly seek unto the Lord's enemy, the devil, is the grossest crime yet.

Nothing could be more vile than the overt practice of demonism. Saul could not afford to compound his judgment by adding this to his other sins. If God was withdrawn from him, he should have been even more afraid of increasing the Lord's wrath by consulting a necromancer. Instead, he rushes forward into this sin, driven by passion instead of by principle.

Saul and two servants went *incognito* to this woman that had a familiar spirit. She was a medium, or a trance-channeler of departed spirits. Upon contact with the spirit world, an evil spirit would impersonate the dead through the medium of this woman of Endor. In other words, the person making inquiry would not actually contact the deceased, but would presumably receive a message from the departed dead through the medium (cf. Ecc. 9:5-6).

When Saul requested that she bring up Samuel, however, something happened that she by her demonic rituals had never seen before. She was clearly startled (v. 12) and being in a state of clairvoyance, she immediately recognized Saul beneath his disguise, an indication of the supernatural powers at work on this occasion.

Her surprise at Samuel's appearance indicates that something other than demonic power was at work here. God, who rules both heaven and hell, allowed Samuel to appear to announce one final message of doom to the unhappy king (see Ezek. 14:4, 7-8).

What did Samuel say? Two things: (1) Israel will suffer defeat in tomorrow's battle; (2) Saul and his sons would die in the battle (v. 19).

Upon hearing the dreadful sentence, Saul fainted to the ground in fear and trembling. There would be no stay of execution this time. As he lay prostrate on the floor of the witch's house, she compelled him to eat what would prove to be his last meal.

Unhappy man! Look where his sins have brought him—to the home of a devil worshipper, abandoned by God and sentenced to die by the very man who had once anointed him as king of Israel. Alas! How the mighty have fallen, indeed!

Chapter 15
In the Ruins of Ziklag
1 Samuel 29-30

First Samuel 29-30 provides another example of God's restraining providence. Having joined himself to the king of Gath, David finds himself in the precarious position of joining the Philistine army in battle against his own people Israel.

Though he had previously refused to lift his hand against God's anointed king, had God now totally abandoned him to the consequences of his own foolish choices, he would have inevitably lifted his hand to do harm to God's anointed people. How mercifully our God deals with his servants to protect them even from their own indiscretions!

Disappointment - His Appointment

It is evident in chapter 29 that David is no longer thinking clearly. When the "lords of the Philistine" army voiced distrust for David, he acted as though he had been hurt. *"What have I done ...that I may not go fight against the enemies of my lord the king?"* he asks (1 Sam. 29:8).

Whether he is genuinely disappointed because of a legitimate desire to fight against Israel, or merely attempting to keep up his masquerade of loyalty for the sake of being consistent, or expressing his carnal pride because of the sting to his ego that rejection had brought, David is talking himself into trouble.

In spite of himself, however, God intends to close the door to what would prove to be a catastrophic step. Could it be that David would have encountered Jonathan, or his own brother Eliab or Abinidab or Shammah in the battle?

How mercifully God spared him the treachery of that moment!

How many times have you looked back with 20/20 hindsight on a moment of disappointment and prayed, "Thank you Lord that I was not permitted to have what I wanted"? The Heavenly Father knows what is best for his children and in his mercy and wisdom, withholds his permission from those things that would be to their and his dishonor even when they do not have the sense to judge what is right. Sometimes, disappointment is indeed His appointment.

Cast Down but Not Destroyed

Dejected and disillusioned, David and his army headed home to Ziklag. What he doesn't know is that God is dealing with him to bring him to repentance by means of the embarrassment of being distrusted and rejected and now, by isolating him even from his own men.

As the soldiers neared camp, they noticed that Ziklag was a smoking ruin. A band of Amalekite marauders had invaded the unguarded camp, burned it with fire, and kidnapped the women and children. At this sight, the already discouraged army wept until they could weep no more.

"And David was greatly distressed; for the people spoke of stoning him, because the soul of all the people was grieved, every man for his sons and for his daughters." (1 Sam. 30:6). David's loyal soldiers, now disappointed in him as their leader, consider putting him to death. No wonder he was "greatly distressed." He had let the men down. He should have anticipated that an unguarded camp would be an easy target for the Amalekites, eager to revenge David's recent campaign against them.

Why hadn't he left a garrison of soldiers to protect the families while the men were away? A leader should have prepared for all eventualities. Further, David had a sense of personal loss, for both Abigail and Ahinoam were gone. To top it all they had no hope of recovering their captives, for David and his men were afoot, but the raiders were traveling by horseback and camel. Ah! What a pitiful sight is the lonely fugitive standing there in the ruins of Ziklag!

But was this the end? Had the many years of wilderness wanderings come to this? Were all the mighty displays of Divine providence he had experienced for naught? These questions must have echoed in the dejected warrior's mind until faith sprang up afresh like flowers in the springtime. Then, *"David encouraged himself in the Lord his God"* (1 Sam. 30:6b).

As he began to meditate on the character of God, he found new courage and hope. Surely the man who wrote so many of the Psalms must have reminded himself of their truths concerning God's sovereignty, faithfulness, mercy, wisdom, majesty and grace.

No doubt he reviewed God's mighty acts in human history as recorded in the Pentateuch. And what about his own experience of deliverance after deliverance from the hand of God? He encouraged himself in the Lord "his" God.

Standing in the ruins of Ziklag, David turned back to the God who had carried him safe thus far, and once again God showed himself strong in David's desperation. When the victims were all recovered and the soldiers were returned home, David penned the words to Psalm 18.

Psalm 18

A Psalm of David, the servant of the LORD, who spake unto the LORD the words of this song in the day that the LORD delivered him from the hand of all his enemies, and from the hand of Saul: And he said,

I will love thee, O LORD, my strength.
The LORD is my rock, and my fortress, and my deliverer;
my God, my strength, in whom I will trust;
my buckler, and the horn of my salvation,
and my high tower.
I will call upon the LORD, who is worthy to be praised:
so shall I be saved from mine enemies.
The sorrows of death compassed me,
and the floods of ungodly men made me afraid.
The sorrows of hell compassed me about:
the snares of death prevented me.
In my distress I called upon the LORD, and cried unto my God:
he heard my voice out of his temple,
and my cry came before him, even into his ears…
For by thee I have run through a troop;
and by my God have I leaped over a wall.
As for God, his way is perfect:
the word of the LORD is tried:
he is a buckler to all those that trust in him.
For who is God save the LORD?
or who is a rock save our God?
It is God that girdeth me with strength,
and maketh my way perfect.
He maketh my feet like hinds' feet,
and setteth me upon my high places.
He teacheth my hands to war,
so that a bow of steel is broken by mine arms.
Thou hast also given me the shield of thy salvation:
and thy right hand hath holden me up
and thy gentleness hath made me great.
Thou hast enlarged my steps under me,

> that my feet did not slip.
> I have pursued mine enemies, and overtaken them:
> neither did I turn again till they were consumed.
> I have wounded them that they were not able to rise:
> they are fallen under my feet.
> For thou hast girded me with strength unto the battle:
> thou hast subdued under me
> those that rose up against me…
> Thou hast delivered me from the strivings of the people;
> and thou hast made me the head of the heathen:
> a people whom I have not known shall serve me.
> As soon as they hear of me, they shall obey me:
> the strangers shall submit themselves unto me…
> The LORD liveth; and blessed be my rock;
> and let the God of my salvation be exalted.
> It is God that avengeth me,
> and subdueth the people under me.
> He delivereth me from mine enemies:
> yea, thou liftest me up above those that rise up against me:
> thou hast delivered me from the violent man.
> Therefore will I give thanks unto thee, O LORD, among the heathen,
> and sing praises unto thy name.
> Great deliverance giveth he to his king;
> and sheweth mercy to his anointed
> to David, and to his seed for evermore.

Chapter 16
Tell it not in Gath
1 Samuel 31 - 2 Samuel 1

Perhaps no scene in David's life more clearly reveals the nobility of his heart than the closing scene of the wilderness years. Protected by God from what would prove to be a catastrophic battle between the Philistines and Israel, David responds with grace and pathos to the news that Saul and Jonathan had been slain.

Saul's Death

From the beginning of the battle, the Philistines routed Israel. Saul watched his men perish one after another on Mount Gilboa (v. 1). Then he saw his sons Jonathan, Abinadab, and Melchishua slain (v. 2).

Just then, Saul himself was mortally wounded by the Philistine archers. He begged his armor-bearer to put an end to his life, but he would not. Saul then drew his own sword and fell upon it lest the Philistines should capture and torture him.

The next day, the Philistine soldiers discovered the bodies of Saul and his three sons. They took Saul's armor, displayed it in the temple of their pagan idols, and fastened his body to the wall of Bethshan. The valiant men of Saul's hometown, however, went by night to retrieve the bodies of Saul and his sons, in a display of great respect for their king.

Three days later, an Amalekite messenger came to David at Ziklag. *"How went the matter?"* David asked. The courier reported the massacre and added *"Saul and Jonathan...are dead also"* (2 Sam. 1:4).

When David inquired further, the courier answered in a way that indicated that he expected David to be elated at the news. Undoubtedly, he saw an opportunity to gain David's favor, so he gave Saul's crown and bracelet to David and claimed credit for personally putting an end to Saul. David was anything but happy, however, and ordered the Amalekite to be executed for daring to lift his hand against God's anointed.

David's Song

Then David composed a lament psalm for Saul and Jonathan to be used in the training of the children of Judah (2 Sam. 1:17-27).

Like the Amalekite messenger, we too are surprised at David's reaction to the death of King Saul. We would expect him to rejoice that the man who had tormented him so relentlessly is dead. Instead he mourns.

We are further surprised at the tone and language of the song. We expect David to mention Saul's failures and flaws. Instead he speaks reverently and admirably of the fallen monarch.

Three times he laments in the language of exclamation: *"How are the mighty fallen!"* He pronounces a curse upon the battlefield (v. 21), glories in the fact that the king had fought with valor (v. 22), and calls upon the daughters of Israel to weep over the king under whose regime they had enjoyed many comforts.

Because he wants future generations to think of Saul with dignity and veneration, David depicts the house of Saul at death not in strife and conflict, but in regal togetherness (v. 23). Then, turning his attention to Jonathan, David voices his personal grief and deep affection for his friend. Jonathan, the son of the sitting king, had been loyal to David at a time when David's own wife had abandoned him (v. 26).

To what should we attribute this gracious expression of David's heart? David has a deep respect for the position of God's king and is sensitive to and concerned for the grieving people of Israel.

David, the shepherd-hearted fugitive, is beginning to behave like a king. He knows that the death of a national leader is a heavy blow to the whole nation. Through this hymn, he expresses solidarity with the nation in their grief and the nobility of character that cares more for others than himself. Such selflessness is the noblest of virtues.

Contrary to all expectations, David responds to the tragedy of the hour by reminding God's people not to gossip. *"Tell it not in Gath; publish it not in Askelon, lest the daughters of the uncircumcised triumph"* (v. 20).

Don't talk about it, he says, lest the enemy take the occasion to blaspheme the name of God. Ah! A bitter, vengeful man, he is not. David, this is your finest hour!

Part 2

The Glory Years

2 Samuel 2 – 10

Chapter 17
A Turbulent Transition to the Throne
2 Samuel 2-3

The decade of wandering in the wilderness now comes to a welcome end as David, age thirty (2 Sam. 5:4), begins his forty-year reign over Israel. Instead of marching into Saul's palace and assuming the throne immediately, however, David cautiously and humbly seeks the Lord's guidance, and begins his reign in Hebron. There he stayed for seven and one-half years (2:1-11).

Why did God send him to Hebron rather than Jerusalem? Because all Israel did not yet recognize David as the new king. The men of Judah alone initially acknowledged David as God's choice (2:1-7) and until God was pleased to make His will manifest, David would have to wait on the Lord.

The Turbulence of Civil War

These transition years were extremely turbulent. Saul's youngest and only surviving son, Ishbosheth, because he was the sole heir to the throne, was crowned king by Abner, the highest ranking officer in Saul's army. He reigned for two years over every other tribe except Judah (2:8-10). This act occasioned *"a long war between the house of Saul and the house of David,"* the chief players of which were the two military generals, Abner, Saul's cousin (1 Sam. 14:50), and Joab, David's nephew (1 Chr. 2:16).

At first, Abner & Joab held a summit at the pool of Gibeon, but the suggestion that soldiers from each side engage in a friendly sparring contest quickly turned bloody (2:12-16). Twenty-four young soldiers (twelve from each side) died and the bedlam of all-out war broke out. At the end of the day, David had lost nineteen men plus Asahel, Joab's fleet-footed brother, but Abner's men had lost three hundred sixty.

As time passed, David *"waxed stronger and stronger, and the house of Saul waxed weaker and weaker"* (3:1). It was during this period of growing political strength, however, that the Holy Spirit inserts into the narrative a hint of a personal weakness in David's character.

Beside his wives Ahinoam and Abigail, David took four more wives during his stay in Hebron (3:2-5). These six wives bore him six sons, one of which was a son named Absalom. His polygamy would return to haunt him in many ways over the next 3 ½ decades.

The Turbulence of Politics

Abner had ulterior motives in supporting Ishbosheth as king. He was an ambitious man driven by an unquenchable thirst for personal power. Seeing an opportunity to seize greater control (3:6), Abner took to himself one of Saul's court women, an act of profound political overtones. It was tantamount to an assumption of royal power.

When Ishbosheth confronted him, Abner retaliated by deserting to David. David, however, would not agree to a meeting unless Abner brought Michal, David's wife whom Saul had given to another man.

Knowing that he had no option, Ishbosheth took her from her husband Phaltiel, who followed her all the way to Bahurim, weeping profusely. But Abner was unmoved by the emotion. He did not care how his political ambition might affect others. Michal was just the ticket he needed to win David's favor. *"Go home"* he said to Phaltiel and the man returned (3:7-16).

Before the elders of Israel, Abner said all of the right things, promising to help them make David the king (3:17-21). He didn't know, however, that his days were numbered.

The Turbulence of Revenge

Joab had not forgotten the fact that Abner had killed his brother Asahel. When he heard, therefore, that Abner had made an alliance with David, he was livid. *"Why did you allow him to escape?"* Joab asked. *"Don't you know that he came to deceive you?"*

At that point, Joab decided he must take matters into his own hands (a kind of vigilantism that Joab will exhibit on several occasions as the narrative unfolds). Without David's knowledge, Joab sent for Abner, took him aside for a private conference, and thrust his knife under Abner's fifth rib, to avenge *"the blood of Asahel his brother"* (3:23-27).

This fierce act of revenge grieved the heart of David and the people. He pronounced a curse on the house of Joab (3:29), commanded Joab and Abishai to attend Abner's funeral (3:31), and personally followed the bier to the grave with weeping. When he refused to eat meat while it was day, the people of Israel knew that David was not responsible for Abner's death. And *"whatsoever the king did pleased all the people"* (3:36).

Thus was David, without a self-conscious effort to win the people's favor, growing in popularity, while others who attempted to arrange circumstances to their own advantage were thwarted. Let this remind us that God will upset all of the nice calculations of those who politic for their own advantage. It is in His hand to elevate a person to honor and those who attempt to manufacture their own prestige will eventually be abased.

Unlike Abner who sought his own advantage, and unlike Joab who impetuously resorted to vigilante justice, David was willing to wait patiently for God to remove the obstacles to the throne. Slowly, but surely, in the providence of God, the day of his coronation as King of all Israel was drawing near.

Chapter 18
Coronation Day
2 Samuel 4-5

The assassination of Ishbosheth (2 Sam. 4) was the last dark cloud looming over the landscape of David's long accession to the throne, and as the cloud dissipated, the sun broke through upon his life in an unprecedented way. The next twenty years would be "the glory years" as David became, under the blessing of God, the mightiest monarch in the land.

No enemy army would be able to stand before the king of Israel. During his reign, the territorial boundaries of Israel would be expanded from 6,000 to 60,000 square miles. Further, an extensive network of trade routes would be established that would bring unprecedented wealth into Israel. David's monarchy was indeed glorious. 2 Samuel 5 describes the beginning of the glory years.

Reunification of the People

The glory of David's throne started with his coronation. After the death of Ishbosheth, the tribes of Israel submitted to David as king so that all Israel and Judah were once more united (vs. 1-5). This was an unspeakably happy day with enthusiasm at a fevered pitch.

First Chronicles 12:23-40 records that literally thousands of soldiers marched spontaneously to Hebron from the most remote parts of the country, bringing with them various gifts to be used in the three-day feast on this joyous occasion. The grand total of warriors that appeared in Hebron was 339,600 men and 1,222 tribal chiefs. What a significant display of national unity as David was anointed king over all Israel and Judah!

Relocation of the Throne

"Surrounded by a force of such magnitude and enthusiasm, David must have felt that this was the proper moment for the greatest undertaking in Jewish history since the conquest of the land under Joshua. The first act of David's government must appropriately be the conquest of Israel's capital"[1].

Second Samuel 5:6-12 records the relocation of the throne to Jerusalem. Because the stronghold on Mout Zion was held by the Jebusites, the relocation of the national capital would require a battle.

Mount Zion was so naturally fortified that the Jebusites taunted David saying, *"David cannot come in hither, for even the blind and the lame will drive him away"* (v. 6). *"Nevertheless, David took the stronghold of Zion"* (v. 7), for no conquest was too difficult for God.

Once he was settled in Jerusalem, *"David perceived that the Lord had established him king over Israel, and that he had exalted his kingdom for his people Israel's sake"* (v. 12). The long anticipated day had finally arrived when David would awake one morning and say, "God has fulfilled his promise and established me as king." This was a day of inexpressibly sweet confirmation.

Restoration of Military Dominance

Unlike Saul, who early-on allowed his position of power to corrupt his character, David did not let his new position of prominence and popularity "go to his head." When the Philistines thought that the new king's coronation provided a fresh opportunity to rout the Israelites, David inquired of the Lord, saying, *"Shall I go up to the Philistines?"* (v. 19). The Lord replied, *"Go up, for I will doubtless deliver the Philistines into thine hand."* When he smote them, he gave the glory to God saying, *"The Lord hath broken forth upon mine enemies before me, even as the breach of waters"* (v. 20).

The Philistines then launched a second attack. David inquired of the Lord a second time, but this time the Lord commanded a different tactic. *"Go behind them...and when you hear the sound of a going in the tops of the mulberry trees, then thou shalt bestir thyself: for then shall the Lord go out before thee, to smite the...Philistines"* (vs. 22-24). David obeyed and won a categorical victory.

Though he was king and commander of the Israelite army, David knew that Jehovah was the real King. Unlike Saul, King David humbly took his orders from the Lord and the Lord showed himself strong on behalf of his obedient servant.

The key element of David's "glory years" was his readiness to acknowledge that God had established him king and that God was the ultimate Sovereign over the land. All Israel might now sing, "Happy times are here again!"

---

[1] Alfred Edersheim, *Bible History: Old Testament*, Vol.4, p.166

Chapter 19
Recovering the Lost Ark
2 Samuel 6

After his victory over the Philistines, king David sought to restore the true worship of God from the sad state to which devotion to God had declined during Saul's monarchy. The ark of the covenant, once captured by the Philistines (1 Sam. 4:11), had stayed in the house of Abinadab for sixty-five years (1 Sam. 7:1) and *"no one had inquired any more at it in the days of Saul"* (1 Chr. 13:3).

A general complacency toward the worship of God prevailed. The restoration of a national worship revolving around God's tabernacle, therefore, was of first importance. The ark must be brought home again.

A Passion for God's Glory (vs. 1-2)

Consumed by his zeal to reestablish tabernacle worship, David summoned thirty thousand chosen men of Israel together and communicated to them the vision that filled his heart. It would be a monumental undertaking, but God's ark belonged in the Holy of Holies, not in the house of Abinadab. Persuaded by his arguments, the men committed to the mission (1 Chr. 13:2-3a).

Why was the ark so important'? This holy piece of furniture had been constructed at the express command and according to the exact specifications of God (Ex. 25). It symbolically represented the presence of God in the midst of his people. This holy box contained the tables of the Law, Aaron's rod that budded, and the golden pot of manna, reminders of God's holy precepts, priestly caste, and providential blessings.

It was a sort of icon, therefore, of everything that was essential to their national history and community life. The ark represented their identity as the people of God. Further, the mercy seat, the lid of the ark, was sprinkled with blood by the High Priest on the annual Day of Atonement. It was, therefore, central to the worship of God.

A Reminder of God's Holiness (vs. 3-11)

The late Vance Havner said, "God's work must be done by God's people in God's way." On this occasion, God's people were doing God's work, but, in their haste to "get the job done," they failed to do it God's way. The result of their pragmatism was tragic.

They constructed a new cart for the purpose of transporting the ark to Jerusalem. One wonders if they borrowed this idea from the Philistines (see 1 Sam 6:7). Two oxen steered by Uzzah and Ahio, the sons of Abinadab, drew the cart.

As the procession began, a spirit of festive joy prevailed (v. 5). Suddenly, one of the oxen stumbled. Uzzah instinctively reached forth to steady the tipping ark, but as his hand made contact with the holy box, *"the anger of the Lord was kindled against Uzzah; and God smote him there for his error [lit. rashness]; and there he died by the ark of God"* (v. 7).

At once the procession halted and the music stopped. The people were surprised with terror. What began as a celebration had suddenly turned to a catastrophe. Even *"David was displeased [lit. angry and indignant]" with the Lord* (v. 8).

Are we, like David, surprised at the severity of the punishment? Does God's reaction appear to be extreme?

Do we think that Uzzah deserved a reward for 'saving the day' rather than such a stroke of Divine judgment?

Let it be remembered, then, that God's specific commandments regarding the transportation and treatment of the ark had been ignored. The Mosaic Law required that the ark be carried on staves by Levites, not conveyed on the backs of oxen by two boys who were not even of the tribe of Aaron. Further, it was to be born on staves (sticks), without direct human contact, "lest they die" (Num. 4:15; 7:9).

Uzzah's zeal, notwithstanding its possible good intention, was presumptuous and unholy. Through negligence of God's worship, the people had become careless and irreverent in their attitude toward God's law. God aimed to remind them, in this very distinct way, that he intends to be taken seriously. They must never trifle with him. Had they done it God's way in the first place, no tragedy would have occurred.

Krummacher states, "For an everlasting memorial that the Lord is a 'jealous God', who will not suffer the least violation of any one of his commandments, David called the place where the death-stroke fell down on Uzzah's head, Perez-uzzah (i.e., the 'rent of Uzzah')." Paralyzed, then, by the possibility of presuming on God further, David left the ark in the house of Obededom, a Levite, and returned home without it.

But over the next three months, David observed how the Lord blessed the house of Obededom, and took courage to resume his initial plan. This time, however, in holy caution and reverence for God, he did everything strictly "by the book" (v. 13; cf. 1 Chr. 15:2, 12-13).

Uninhibited Joy in God's Worship
(vs. 12-23)

When the Lord's work is done in the Lord's way, the Lord smiles upon the service. Sensing his pleasure and the significance of this monumental occasion, David and the men of Israel were almost euphoric.

The singers sang, and the trumpeters sounded, and David leaped and danced before the Lord with all his might. It was a moment of hallowed and uninhibited joy in the Lord.

David had composed two Psalms for this festive occasion - Psalm 15 and Psalm 24. Psalm 15 reflects the attitude of reverential fear due to God in worship, an attitude rediscovered no doubt by means of the breach upon Uzzah. Psalm 24 reflects the attitude of jubilant worship as the gates of the city swung wide to welcome back her real Conqueror and King, *"Jehovah mighty in battle, the King of glory."* Ah, the pure delight of this festive hour!

As the procession moved into the city, however, the harmony of joy was interrupted by a dissonant note. Just at that moment, Michal, David's wife, came to the window and viewed her husband's radiant face. Here he was, the king of Israel, dressed not in royal garb, in the midst of the commoners behaving in this undignified manner. And Michal *"despised him in her heart"* (v. 16). Obviously, she did not share his joy in the Lord.

After personally leading the large crowd in a thanksgiving feast, David returned to share the joy with his household. But Michal met him at the door with her word of scorn, *"How glorious was the king of Israel today, who uncovered himself today in the eyes of the handmaidens of his servants, as one of the vain fellows shamelessly uncovereth himself!"* (v. 20).

Undaunted, David replied in effect, "I was worshipping God, not trying to please man." He refused to let anyone, even his wife, rob him of the joy of worship, or hinder him from expressing his gratitude to God for his many mercies. His stern rebuke to this one who aimed to steal his joy in the Lord serves to remind us of the need to seek, beyond all else, to please and glorify our God, regardless of what others think. Yes, we pity the poor woman, whose own pride has brought her to the point where she can no longer recognize the blessing of God upon his people.

And, we admire the man after God's own heart, whose love and gratitude to God caused him to celebrate God's grace in uninhibited worship. *"Look to yourselves, brethren, that you lose not those things that you have wrought, but that you receive a full reward"* (2 Jno. 3).

Chapter 20
The House that God Builds
2 Samuel 7

It is not possible to "out-give" the Lord. His grace always exceeds man's gratitude. Thankful people, however, must try. Compelled by an overwhelming sense of the Lord's goodness, David felt an inescapable urge to do something for the Lord.

In 2 Samuel 7 we learn, however, that our gifts of gratitude cannot compare with God's gifts of grace. The sinner's hope arises from what God does for him, not what he does for the Lord.

A Great Passion

After many years of conflict, God gave David *"rest from all his enemies"* (v.1) for a season. These were the best of times. With peace in his home and nation, David reflected on the blessings of God.

At once he thought of the ark of God: *"I dwell in a house of cedar, but the ark of God dwelleth within curtains"* (v. 2). It was in David's heart to build a permanent abode for God's ark, a temple for the honor of the Lord's name.

He was not motivated by personal ambition, but by a genuine desire to glorify God and God was pleased that David wanted to build a house for Him (1 Kings 8:17-18). Even Nathan the prophet encouraged him to proceed: *"Go, do all that is in thine heart; for the Lord is with thee"* (v. 3).

A Greater Power

Even though David's desire was noble, God would not permit it. He sent Nathan to David with the disappointing news. Because the city was not yet secure from war (1

Kings 5:3-4) and because he had shed blood abundantly in battle (1 Chr. 22:7-8), David was not permitted to construct the temple.

David must acquiesce to the sovereignty of God. But even in disappointment, the Lord mercifully allowed David to begin stockpiling materials for the future temple and revealed that David's son would be permitted to fulfill David's dream.

The Greatest Promise

His momentary disappointment must have quickly dissolved as Nathan uttered a single sentence: David, you wanted to build the Lord a house, but now *"the Lord telleth thee that He will make thee a house"* (v. 11). David desired to do something great for the Lord, but God will do something even greater for David.

That which follows in verses 12-16 is called the Davidic Covenant. In this solemn oath, God unconditionally pledges to establish his kingdom forever and to never remove his *mercy* [lit. Heb. *chesed* means covenant loyalty] from David's son.

It is a unilateral covenant, the obligation for fulfilling its provisions resting solely on God. Though the immediate application is to Solomon, these prophetic promises apply ultimately to the Lord Jesus Christ, "David's greater Son" (Lk. 1:32-33; Acts 2:29-30; Rev. 22:16). It is because of God the Father's covenant with the Lord Jesus Christ that all of God's people, sinners though they be, have eternal security (Ps. 89:27-37).

Is it any wonder that when he came to die, David looked for comfort not to the things he had accomplished for God, but to God's covenant provisions to him? *"Now these be the last words of David...Although my house be not so with God, yet He hath made with me an everlasting covenant, ordered in all things and sure: for this is all my salvation, and all my desire, although He make it not to grow"* (2 Sam. 23:5). With unrealized dreams regarding the house he wanted to build for the Lord, David was not the least bit disappointed in the house that God had built for him.

The house that God builds for all of His children is an eternal building, a house not made with hands, eternal in the heavens (2 Cor. 5:1). It is the city that He has prepared for the objects of His eternal love. It is a mansion in the Father's house with the entire redeemed family. It is a house in which He has made the provision and in which all of His little ones will forever rest secure and satisfied in His love.

That's the house that God builds. Whatever you would do for Him to show your gratitude will never begin to compare with what He has already done for you and for the entire covenant family by His amazing grace.

Chapter 21
David The Great
2 Samuel 8

Second Samuel 8 depicts David at the pinnacle of his greatness. It records the expansion of his kingdom under God's blessing, cataloging five major military victories (over the Philistines, Moabites, the region of Zobah, the Syrians [or Aramaens], and the Edomites). With the further record of his victory over the Ammonites (2 Sam. 10), David's territorial boundaries were expanded from six to sixty thousand square miles.

Conquering His Enemies

Idolatrous heathen tribes surrounded David's kingdom: the Philistines & Edomites on the south, the Moabites and Ammonites to the east, and the Syrians in the region of Zobah to the north. Each posed a hostile threat to the people of God.

The first victory recorded was David's triumph over Israel's archenemy, the Philistines (v. 1). In this categorical defeat and total subjugation of the Philistines, David seized control of the mother city, Gath (cf. 1 Chr. 18:1). This is the region known in the modern world as "the West Bank."

Interestingly, archaeologists state that Philistine civilization mysteriously disappeared during David's reign. After his tenure on the throne, the Philistines, as a nation, are never heard from again.

Next, the Moabites invaded from the east but David prevailed. He slew two-thirds of the Moabite soldiers, sparing one-third of the army to serve as indentured servants (v.2).

Then Hadadezer of Zobah, the most powerful king of the Syrian princes, attempted to recover his territory at the River Euphrates. The tribe of Reuben had gained control of this area during the reign of Saul. Again, however, David defeated the armed revolt (v. 3-4).

Other Syrian princes joined Hadadezer, but David slew 22,000 men and took the remainder as servants. He also occupied the chief cities of Syria and dedicated all of the spoils of the battle to the Lord (vs. 5-8, 11-12). According to 1 Chronicles 18:8, Solomon used the brass David had accumulated as spoil from these battles to construct the brazen laver, the brass pillars and other articles of brass in the temple.

One Syrian prince, however, Toi king of Hamath, refused to join the others to reinforce Hadadezer. Because of a long standing conflict with Hadadezer. Toi was pleased by the news of David's victory. He sent his son to congratulate David with many more vessels of gold, silver, and brass. David also consecrated the metal from all of these for use in the service of the Lord (vs. 9-12).

Thinking that David was preoccupied by the Syrian wars, the Edomites invaded from the south. According to Psalm 60, composed by David during this particular battle, Israel suffered some temporary setbacks. But under the leadership of Joab and Abishai (cf. Ps. 60 "Title" and 1 Chr. 18:12), David pushed the Edomites back to the Valley of Salt and slew 18,000 men. The victory was so significant that *"David got him a name"* (vs. 13-14). Perhaps he became known as "David the Great"!

What was the secret to David's military success? To what should we attribute his reputation for greatness?

Perhaps it was due in part to the greatness of his army. It was during these several campaigns that David's mighty men performed numerous exploits, as recorded in 2 Samuel 23. Yes, he had a number of talented and mighty soldiers.

Saul also had a number of courageous soldiers, yet he was never held in reputation like David. The key to David's military achievements was not his personal skill or the valor of his commanding officers. Rather, twice in the narrative, the Holy Spirit says, *"The Lord preserved David whithersoever he went"* (vs. 6, 14).

In a word, God's blessing is what made David great. David's great success and great power over his enemies was the result of the greatness of David's God. Because of God's covenant commitment to David, the Lord fought his battles. It was Jehovah alone that tread down David's enemies (Ps. 60:12). And David was not reluctant to acknowledge that fact.

Psalms 20 and 108 are also Davidic war-songs composed during the same period as Psalm 60. Each expresses confidence in the God of Israel as the sole source of victory. And each suggests that God had not only made David a great king, and a great soldier, but He had also given him a great heart.

Psalm 108

A Song of Psalm of David.

O God, my heart is fixed;
I will sing and give praise, even with my glory...
Be thou exalted, O God, above the heavens:
and thy glory above all the earth;
That thy beloved may be delivered:

save with thy right hand, and answer me.
God hath spoken in his holiness; I will rejoice, I will divide Shechem,
and mete out the valley of Succoth.
Gilead is mine; Manasseh is mine; Ephraim also is the strength of mine head; Judah is my lawgiver; Moab is my washpot; over Edom will I cast out my shoe; over Philistia will I triumph.
Who will bring me into the strong city?
Who will lead me into Edom?
Wilt not thou, O God, who has cast us off?
And wilt not thou, O God, go forth with our hosts?
Give us help from trouble: for vain is the help of man.
Through God we shall do valiantly:
for he it is that shall tread down our enemies.

Chapter 22
Kings, Cripples, and Kindness
2 Samuel 9

In this chapter, David's glory displays itself not only in military dominance or material riches, but in personal benevolence and grace. David's readiness to stoop to show kindness to an inferior, even one who might be perceived as his enemy, is one of the most vivid examples of grace in the Old Testament.

As such, it is also one of the most powerful illustrations of God's grace to sinners in Christ in the entire Bible. In the story of Mephibosheth, we may see reflected as in a mirror our own autobiographical images.

A King's Initiative

"And David said, Is there yet any that is left of the house of Saul that I may show him kindness for Jonathan's sake?" (v. 1). This strange inquiry, appearing suddenly in the narrative of David's royal and military greatness, captures the very essence of the definition of grace. *Grace* is God's initiative to bestow favor moved by nothing but His own sovereign love.

What could have possibly motivated this important king to think of extending favor to others? What external circumstance might have prompted him to want to show kindness to the house of the former king? Compelled by nothing outside himself but by his own love for Jonathan, David seeks to fulfill the vow he made to show mercy to Saul's house.

A Crippled Man's Fear

"Now when Mephibosheth...was come to David, he fell on his face...and he bowed himself and said, What is thy servant, that thou shouldest look upon such a dead dog as I am?" (vs. 6, 8). The last surviving descendant of Saul was the lame-footed son of Jonathan named Mephibosheth.

Injured when his nurse dropped the five-year old while fleeing for safety (2 Sam. 4:4), Mephibosheth had lived low-profile in the house of Machir in Lodebar. Oriental kings tended to look at the surviving heirs of their predecessor as potential threats to the throne; consequently, it was natural for Mephibosheth to fear for his safety, even for his life, once David assumed the crown.

On this occasion, he must have wondered, "What possible motive would the King have in issuing a summons to me? I cannot be a valiant soldier in his army. I have neither wealth nor wisdom for service in his royal court. What use can I be with this marred and mangled body? Surely he intends to slay me."

A Monarch's Kindness

"And David said unto him, Fear not: for I will surely show thee kindness for Jonathan thy father's sake, and will restore thee all the land of Saul ...and thou shalt eat bread at my table continually" (v. 7). To the lame man's surprise, David extends to him not retributive justice but redeeming grace. He stooped, in condescending mercy, to receive in the welcome embrace of fellowship the maimed and deformed grandson of Saul.

Why? Why would David suddenly reach out to favor this handicapped man? Not because of anything noteworthy or meritorious in Mephibosheth, but because he loved his father Jonathan.

David "showed kindness" to him. This Hebrew word *chesed* is one of the great words of the Old Testament. It means covenant loyalty and faithful love. Though Mephibosheth had every reason to anticipate David's wrath, instead he received David's loyal love, "for Jonathan's sake."

A Personal Application

Why does God save sinners? What motive would possibly compel Him to rescue people who by nature are His enemies, adopt them into his family, and permit them continuous access to His royal table?

Certainly there is nothing in man to commend him to God's favor. Like Mephibosheth, we are crippled in our souls. Deformed by sin, we are not lovely or worthy of the Divine notice. Our daily walk reveals the limp of a fallen nature, a sinful lame-footedness that serves as nothing more than an embarrassing spectacle.

God's favor is extended to sinners solely because of His love for the Lord Jesus Christ. Our sins are forgiven "for Christ's sake" (Eph. 4:32). Because of the covenant with His only begotten Son, God has drawn us to Himself, rescued us from the misery of a life of fear, and permitted us to enjoy a bountiful feast at his table continually, hiding our uncomely parts beneath the table of mercy. Amazing Grace!

Chapter 23
Play the Man!
2 Samuel 10

Chapter ten continues the series of conquests detailed in chapter eight in which David greatly extended and strengthened his kingdom. It describes the most dangerous and fearful of all Israel's wars, i.e. the battle against the Ammonites.

When David received the news that Nahash, king of the Ammonites, was dead, he purposed to show kindness to Hanun, his son, because Nahash had given David help during his wilderness wanderings. David sent servants, therefore, to Nahash *"to comfort him"* (v. 2).

His intentions, however, were misinterpreted and his servants were mocked and insulted (vs. 3-5). Knowing that David would necessarily be provoked by their malicious treatment of his servants, the Ammonites hired an army of more than 30,000 Syrian reinforcements and mounted an attack on Israel (v. 6). Because of the sheer number of auxiliaries the Ammonites were able to engage against Israel, this was the greatest danger yet to threaten David's kingdom.

David countered by sending Joab and the choicest of all his troops to meet them. The Ammonites held their position near Rabbah, their chief fortified city, and the Syrians stood at a distance of about fifteen miles to the southwest (1 Chr. 19:7).

Joab, understanding that he was shut in between two armies, divided Israel into two groups and placed his brother Abishai in command over the one with the instruction, *"If the Syrians be too strong for me, then thou shalt help me: but if the children of Ammon be too strong for thee, then I will come and help thee. Be of good courage, and let us play the men for our people, and for the cities of our God: and the Lord do that which seemeth him good"* (vs. 11-12).

The soldiers had every reason to fight valiantly. They fought for their families, for the safety of their communities, and for the glory of the city of God. They fought with a manly courage that arose from the knowledge that God was in sovereign control, and the Lord gave them the victory.

As the Syrian soldiers fled before Joab, the Ammonites retreated into Rabbah and closed the gates behind them. Joab returned to Jerusalem. The battle, however, was not yet over. Hadad-Ezer recruited more forces from Syria and placed Shobach, a brave and experienced captain, in command.

Another battle was fought at Helam, but this time, David won a categorical victory, slaying over 40,000 soldiers and Shobach, the commander of the rebel forces. The result was that the Syrians signed a treaty of peace with Israel and became tributary unto David. They were henceforth hesitant to help the Ammonites against Israel.

The winter interrupted the war with Ammon, but when spring-time returned, David sent Joab to resume the war by besieging Rabbah (11:1). With the conquest of Rabbah, Ammon was defeated and the borders of Israel were finally secure from enemy invasion.

Psalm 68 was written in connection with the victory over the Ammonites. In its sacred lines, David celebrates the glorious triumph that God wrought for Israel. In animated strains, the Psalmist calls the people to reflect on all God's deliverances and to *"ascribe strength unto God whose excellency is over Israel...[and who] giveth strength and power unto His people"* (vs. 34-35).

The 68th Psalm, however, is more than a celebration of Jehovah's conquests over Israel's political enemies, for the Psalmist also anticipates the ultimate victory in which Messiah would ascend on high, having "led captivity captive," (v. 18), having spoiled all principalities and powers and might and dominion, making a show of them openly and triumphing over them in his death. With such a mighty Sovereign over us, let us in this our day also "play the men for our people and for the city of our God."

Part 3

Turmoil in David's House

2 Samuel 11 – 1 Kings 1

Chapter 24
David's Desecration
2 Samuel 11

Mark Twain once said, "We are all like the moon; we all have a dark side." Those who understand the doctrine of total depravity know he is correct. This chapter records the account of David's great sin, the darkest blot on his illustrious life and career. It shows us the eminently consecrated king of Israel at his lowest, desecrated by unbridled lust coupled with unconscionable deception and treachery.

But lest we are tempted to view the chapter from a distance, with sordid intrigue yet arrogant self-righteousness, let us remember that 2 Samuel 11 is a mirror of our own depraved, "Jeckel & Hyde" hearts. This is, in the final analysis, a story about us and a warning to all who would elevate any sinful creature to the level that belongs only to the Holy God.

For twenty years, David has reigned gloriously over Israel. As spring blossoms, he sends Joab to Rabbah to finish the battle with the Ammonites interrupted by the winter.

Instead of leading the army himself, however, this time David decides to stay behind at Jerusalem (v. 1). That decision would prove to be the hinge on which David's life would turn for the worst. For the next twenty years, David would have turmoil in his house.

A Heart Unguarded (vs. 1-4)

Great sins are seldom if ever committed whimsically. A sinful act, in other words, is generally more than a 'spur-of-the-moment' impulse or freak notion. Usually, the act itself is the product of a heart that has been secretly eroding for some time.

In his unbroken military success, personal comfort, and unprecedented popularity with the people, David had allowed himself to forget his own weakness and vulnerability. Little by little, he settled into the routines of power and luxury. As he became increasingly familiar with success, more and more tensions relaxed. With all of his enemies conquered, David's kingdom was now totally secure from the threat of invasion. His heart, however, was not. David was losing his sensitivity to God.

Bored and idle, David walked on the palace balcony. Just then, his wandering eye beheld a very beautiful woman on a nearby rooftop. His attraction became a fixation and David began to arrange circumstances for the fulfillment of his illicit passion.

To what extent is Bathsheba culpable? Probably as much as David. She was indiscreet. She accepted the invitation to come to the palace. She betrayed her marriage vows. But David was certainly the aggressor. It was, clearly, a mutual episode, a momentary fling, but it had monumental consequences. The pleasure of the moment was soon replaced by the pain of reproach, for Bathsheba was pregnant.

A Conscience Silenced (vs. 6-13)

To squash the potential scandal that imperiled his kingdom, David conspired to cover-up his sin. He opted for deception, not confession.

Summoning Uriah home from the battlefield, David feigned concern for the man whose wife he had stolen. He prepared a great feast for Uriah, talked about the battle, and encouraged him to take a needed military leave.

"Go home to your wife and comfort yourself" urged David. But Uriah slept on the palace steps, for he was too loyal to his nation, his God, and his comrades to justify a personal indulgence while the battle raged. What a powerful, albeit unintentional, rebuke to the indulgent king!

Plan two involved impairing Uriah with strong drink, which David did. But still, Uriah would not return home. His plans frustrated and his conscience hardened by panic, David then did the unthinkable.

A Loyalty Betrayed (vs. 14-25)

David sent the unsuspicious warrior back to Joab with his own death-warrant in hand. Written by the same pen with which he had penned his psalms, David ordered treachery. *"Put Uriah in the front of the battle, in the hottest part, and then withdraw that he may be slain."*

The unscrupulous general complied with David's unconscionable decree and Uriah the Hittite, one of David's mighty men (2 Sam. 23:39), died. David committed murder by proxy. He betrayed the loyalty of one of his most valiant soldiers.

When a messenger brought the mournful news of the battle with the single sentence *"Uriah the Hittite is dead also,"* David, who historically lamented the deaths of men like Saul and Abner, made no mention of the Living God, but replied with uncharacteristic appeal to blind fate: *"...the sword devoureth one as well as another..."*

A God Offended (vs. 26-27)

No sooner were the days of mourning ended, than David took Bathsheba as his wife and brought her to the palace. *"But the thing that David had done displeased the Lord"* (v. 27).

The eyes of the Lord behold the children of men and there is no respect of persons with him. David had broken at least five of the Ten Commandments: *"Thou shalt not kill...commit adultery...steal...bear false witness against thy neighbor...covet thy neighbor's wife."*

Because covetousness is idolatry (Col. 3:5), he had also breached commandment number one. Sin is not without its consequences. David would certainly reap the bitter harvest, for God was sorely displeased.

Chapter 25
Thou art the Man!
2 Samuel 12

Who comes to mind when you hear the title "the penitent thief"? Most people, of course, think of the malefactor who was crucified with Jesus.

Centuries prior to the cross, however, there was another "penitent thief." His name was King David. The prose of 2 Samuel 12 coupled with the poetry of Psalm 51 and Psalm 32 provide a veritable theology of repentance.

Confrontation (vs. 1-9)

Nathan the prophet was commissioned by God to awaken David's slumbering conscience. It must have been an unnerving commission, but faithful to His God, he carried it forth.

He did it by the use of a parable. He related a story to the King regarding a rich man, with a great herd, and a poor man, who had nothing but one little ewe lamb. When the rich man entertained a guest one day, he took his neighbor's one ewe lamb to dress for the traveler.

David was indignant. "Such an insensitive and pitiless thief deserves to die," he raged. How could something so treacherous and unjust happen in his kingdom?

"And Nathan said to David, 'Thou art the man...Thou hast killed Uriah the Hittite with the sword, and hast taken his wife to be thy wife" (vs. 7. 9). Krummacher says, "If ever a word from human lips fell with crushing weight, and with the illuminating power of a flash of lightning, it was this."

Nathan's parable first revealed the source of David's sin, i.e. a spirit of ingratitude to the God who had loaded him with blessings. Covetousness always arises from ingratitude.

Secondly, it exposed the injustice of David's sin, i.e. contempt for his neighbor. Sin, by its very nature, victimizes others.

Finally, the tactful parable and David's reaction to it reveals the self-deceptive nature of sin. Fallen people are quick to pass judgment on others for the very sins of which they themselves are guilty. Sin blinds us to our own hypocrisy. It makes us imagine that all is well with us and that we are justified to act as judge and jury of others. That is "*the deceitfulness of sin.*"

Consequences (vs. 10-12)

As a consequence of his sin, Nathan uttered the awful sentence, *"The sword shall never depart from thine house...behold, I will raise up evil against thee out of thine own house..."* (vs. 10-12). The subsequent turmoil in David's family would be the harvest reaped from the seeds of lust.

Sin always has consequences. *"Be not deceived; God is not mocked; for whatsoever a man soweth, that shall he also reap. If ye sow to the flesh, ye shall of the flesh reap corruption..."* (Gal. 6:8). God will strip away every smokescreen and "will bring to light the hidden things of darkness, and will make manifest the counsels of the heart."

Furthermore, God said, because the scandalous nature of David's sin gave the enemies of God *"cause to blaspheme,"* the child Bathsheba carried would die (v. 14). Let this teach us that sin dishonors God, robbing Him of glory and, in fact, giving occasion to the wicked to blaspheme his name.

Conviction (Ps. 51)

His crimes exposed by God and his slumbering conscience stabbed wide awake by the staggering threat of judgment, David sorrowed for his sin. Repentance always begins with the sight of sin. The slumbering conscience is jolted awake by the Holy Spirit who says, "Thou art the man," wounding the unsuspecting sinner with godly sorrow and conviction.

Psalm 51, David's penitential psalm written when Nathan exposed his sin with Bathsheba, describes the experience of conviction of sin vividly. *"My sin is ever before me"* wrote David in Psalm 51:3. The sensible sinner cannot seem to escape the sense of his failure. It looms ominously on the horizon of his thoughts; it stares at him when he looks into the mirror; it nags, pesters, and distracts him at each moment of the day. He simply cannot seem to get away from it.

David cries, *"Behold I was shapen in iniquity and in sin did my mother conceive me"* (Ps. 51:5). A sinner under conviction understands in a fresh and new way the corruption and fallenness of his nature. He describes the experience of conviction as something extremely painful, like the breaking of his bones by God (v. 8). He is contrite and broken. His heart is heavy with a new awareness of guilt.

Confession (v. 13)

"And David said unto Nathan, I have sinned against the Lord" (2 Sam. 12:13). Repentance is a godly sorrow for sin that leads to an open acknowledgment and admission of the sin without any attempt to excuse or justify it.

Humiliated and ashamed, David confesses, in ultimate theological categories and with a torrent of uninhibited emotion, *"Against Thee, Thee only, have I sinned and done this evil in Thy sight"* (Ps. 51:3); *"I acknowledge my sin unto thee, and mine iniquity have I not hid. I said, I will confess my transgressions unto the Lord"* (Ps. 32:5).

Confession, the act of agreeing with God (the word itself means "to speak the same thing"), is the prerequisite of forgiveness. The promise of cleansing is contingent on the acknowledgment of, as opposed to the rationalization of, sin (1 Jno. 1:9; Jer. 3:13; Hos. 14:1-4, 8; Pro. 28:13; Ps. 32:6).

Cleansing

His confession involved an acknowledgment that he lacked integrity (Ps. 51:6), a plea for mercy, pardon, and cleansing (Ps. 51:1-2, 9, 14), and a plea for the restoration of God's presence and influence in his life (Ps. 51:10-12). Nathan then uttered the sweet refrain, *"The Lord also hath put away thy sin; thou shalt not die"* (2 Sam. 12:13b).

This pledge of Divine pardon brought him sweet relief. *"Blessed is the man whose transgression is forgiven and whose sin is covered. Blessed is the man unto whom thou wilt not impute iniquity"* (Ps. 32:1-2). For such cleansing may everyone who belongs to the Lord pray in a time when God may be found (Ps. 32:6).

Encouraged by the promise of forgiveness, David began to plead with God with fasting for the life of the child (vs. 15-23). For seven days he ate no bread.

What was he thinking? *"Who can tell whether God will be gracious to me, that the child may live?"* (v. 22). It is appropriate for sinners who have tasted the pardon of God's free grace to hope in His mercy.

On the seventh day, however, the child died. When David perceived that he was dead, he arose, bathed, went to the house of the Lord to worship, and returned home to eat bread.

He explained his actions to curious onlookers by saying, *"While the child lived, there was hope, but now that he is dead, I cannot bring him back."*

Had David now lost hope? Not at all. His hope now was in the resurrection: *"I shall go to him, but he shall not return to me"* (v. 23). Among the many other wonderful things this account teaches, it affirms that forgiveness does not necessarily eliminate the consequences of sin.

Had God then failed to show mercy? No again. Not only had God mercifully extended forgiveness to David, but verses 24-25 indicate that God gave David and Bathsheba another son named Solomon, *"and the Lord loved him"* (v. 24). When Nathan heard the tidings, he called the boy Jedidiah, meaning "beloved of the Lord."

Consecration

One of the lessons we learn from the account of David's repentance concerns the tendency in fallen human beings to look critically at the sins of others though they are blinded to their own. Does the danger of hypocrisy, then, prohibit people who have sinned from passing judgment on the rightness or the wrongness of someone else's behavior? Should the Christian just "live and let live" because, after all, no one is perfect.

Certainly not. In fact, the truly repentant individual who has received God's grace in the forgiveness of his sins will be the first to consecrate himself anew to a life of holiness and to attempt to promote holiness in the lives of others. Notice an interesting verse in Psalm 51: *"Restore unto me the joy of thy salvation...Then will I teach transgressors thy ways; and sinners shall be converted unto Thee"*(vs. 12-13).

Repentance is manifested by a forsaking of the sin in personal life and the unashamed testimony to others of the standards of God's law, the power of God's grace, and the joys of God's service. Forgiven people are powerful instruments in the hand of God to call sinners to repentance.

Elder Mike Ivey says it well: "All true disciples are converted sinners. All converted sinners are penitent. Repentance is the beginning of discipleship. Only penitent sinners are effective witnesses for Christ. This is vitally true with regard to effective church leadership."[1]

---

[1] Michael Ivey, *Repentance in the Pulpit and the Pew*, p. 85.

Chapter 26
Reaping the Whirlwind
2 Samuel 13:1-14:24

The law of the harvest says, *"He that soweth to the flesh shall of the flesh reap corruption"* (Gal. 6:8). Though David had received forgiveness from God, that is, though God had pardoned David's sin, mercifully spared his life, and received him back into fellowship with Himself, yet the grace of God does not negate the law of the harvest.

As a just and wise God, our Heavenly Father not only forgives the sins of His penitent children, He also applies disciplinary measures to correct His erring child. Forensically, confession brings forgiveness, but on a filial level, that is, within the family, the aftermath of sin is inevitable heartache and difficulty.

As a consequence of David's sin, his entire family suffered great scandal. Second Samuel 13-18 is the infamous record of David's family disintegration. It is a story of treachery, deceit, conspiracy, treason, and scandal. David had sown the wind; now he would reap the whirlwind (Hos. 8:7). Neither he nor his government would ever fully recover from the moral shock of his fall.

How are we to understand the sins of incest, murder, and treason within David's family in light of God's sentence *"The sword shall never depart from thy house"*? Was the rape of Tamar by her half-brother Amnon, the subsequent murder of Amnon by Tamar's brother Absalom, and Absalom's revolution against his own father's throne orchestrated by God as punishment for David's sin? Did God condone or even send these treacheries? If so, how is that consistent with what

Scripture reveals concerning the righteous, moral character of God?

Clearly, God cannot be charged with the wicked acts of men (1 Jno. 2:15-16; Jas. 1:13). The tension here is resolved when we remember that God frequently exercises Divine judgment by removing His providential restraint upon one's circumstances. Without the restraining influence of God, fallen people tend toward the most depraved and wretched of behaviors. Left to himself, man inevitably self-destructs.

Alfred Edersheim makes the interesting observation that the turmoil in David's house during the closing years of his reign was connected with a felt and perceptible weakness on his part. He had conspired to sin; now his house is characterized by one conspiracy after another. He had succumbed to the lust of the flesh; now his house is scandalized by sexual sin. He had taken an abundance of wives; now the family is divided by internal strife. David reaped the bitter harvest of his own self-indulgence.

Amnon's Conspiracy (13:1-19)

The whirlwind of domestic evil in the house of David began with Amnon's lust for his half-sister Tamar. Amnon was the eldest son of Ahinoam the Jezreelitess. At the accursed counsel of Jonadab his friend, Amnon pretended to be sick and requested that Tamar be sent to wait upon him. He subsequently violated his sister's virtue, deaf to her plea for honor.

"When David heard of all these things, he was very wroth" (v. 21). In the Septuagint, verse 21 reads, *"But he vexed not the spirit of Amnon, his son, because he loved him, because he was his firstborn."* David was angry, but he did nothing.

Perhaps Edersheim is correct when he comments, "It is difficult to wield a heavy sword with a maimed arm."

Absalom's Conspiracy (13:20-39)

While David passively refused to punish Amnon, Absalom brooded over his sister's disgrace. For two years, he conspired to avenge the irreparable wrong. Then, at the festive time of sheep-shearing on Absalom's property, he put his plan into action.

He invited the king, but the invitation was declined. He then requested that Amnon, because he was heir-apparent to the throne, be sent. David was suspicious, but he eventually gave permission. One gets the impression throughout this narrative that David deliberately avoided the pain of confrontation, though he suspected foul play.

The plot was carried out. Amnon was killed and Absalom fled to his maternal grandfather at Geshur. When tidings came to David, the entire royal house lifted up its voice and wept, and David *"mourned for [Amnon, his firstborn] everyday"* (v. 37). Though the king had permitted Amnon to go unpunished, Absalom was left in banishment for three years.

Joab's Conspiracy (14:1-24)

Seizing an opportunity to protect his own political interests in case Absalom ever secured the throne, Joab, David's general, conspired to coerce David to reconcile with Absalom. He hired a "wise woman" from Tekoah to come before the king with a parable that would appeal to his compassion.

She told a story of family strife. Her two sons had quarreled and the one had killed the other. Now the entire family sought to avenge the blood of the slain by killing the other. Her plea was for mercy. Unless the king interposed on her behalf, she would be deprived of both her sons. Moved by her plight, David vowed to protect the life of her surviving son.

At this, the wise woman tactfully made application of her story to David's own case. She insisted that David's refusal to *"fetch home his banished"* was a harmful precedent to the entire kingdom (v. 13), that the life of the deceased cannot be restored (v. 14a), and that forgiveness was God-like (v. 14b). The Lord does not act so unmercifully to His erring child, she argues.

David perceived that he had been caught by Joab's guile, but seeing that he had already made his decision, he could not recant. He then called Joab and issued the command to restore his fugitive son. But David, perhaps too proud or still suspicious or still pained by the memory of the crime, said, *"Let him turn to his own house, and let him not see my face."* For two more years, Absalom was denied entrance to the palace.

Krummacher states, "This only served the more thoroughly to embitter the heart of the hardened Absalom against his own father...Absalom's heart remained embittered with hatred against his father, and he planned revenge."

Smarting under the sense of Divine chastening, perhaps David at this point penned the words to Psalm 6: *"O Lord, rebuke me not in thine anger, neither chasten me in thy hot displeasure. Have mercy upon me, O Lord; for I am weak: O Lord, heal me; for my bones are vexed. My soul is also sore vexed: but thou, O Lord, how long? Return, O Lord, deliver my soul: oh save me for thy mercies' sake."*

Chapter 27
Absalom Stole the Hearts
2 Samuel 14 – 15

Clearly, David's home was never a priority in his life. He had been too indulgent and passive in the training of his children (cf. 1 Kings 1:6), frequently allowing his affection to rule his judgment.

Now, as a Divine judgment for his sin, God removed providential restraints and permitted David to reap the natural consequences of neglecting his family. Commenting on the effect David's sin had on his family, A. W. Pink says, "How this should speak to the hearts of parents today! If they forsake the paths of righteousness, there is good reason to believe that God will chasten them by suffering their offspring to do likewise. Children in their youth naturally consider the evil example of their parents an excuse why they may follow in their steps, and grown-up ones too are emboldened and confirmed in sin by the sinful conduct of fathers and mothers."

The sad account of David's domestic disharmony now takes a further turn, the heartache of which must have been tremendous. Absalom conspires to seize his father's throne. What sort of young man could affect such a revolution?

Absalom's Rebellion

First, Absalom was physically attractive (14:25-26). Because he was handsome, he was popular. How sad that society tends to value physical beauty above integrity of character!

Secondly, he was proud and fierce. When Joab failed to reply to his summons, Absalom burned his barley field to the ground (14:28-32). He demanded attention and would stop at nothing to have it.

Third, he was presumptuous and impenitent (14:32-33). He played the victim rather than the villain. As far as he was concerned, he had been dealt an injustice by the king. He felt that he deserved an audience and dared to insist upon it, even if it meant he would be killed.

In the fourth place, he was ambitious and unscrupulous (15:1-12). He maneuvered into position to assume David's throne by standing at the gate of the city and flattering the people as they came to the king for judgment. Little by little, he built himself up by tearing the king down. *"So Absalom stole the hearts of the men of Israel"* (15:6).

How did he do so? He flattered the people. Turning on the charm, he played the politician, shaking hands and kissing babies and showing interest in their respective plights and difficulties.

When he perceived that he possessed sufficient political power, Absalom proclaimed himself king (vs. 7-11). Even David's counselor Ahithophel joined the mutiny. *"And the conspiracy was strong; for the people increased continually with Absalom"* (v. 12).

David's Humiliation

The growing popularity of Absalom and the public disenchantment with David resulted in a massive exodus and transfer of allegiance. Politically, David had lost the respect of the people.

Sensing the probability of a *coup d'état* with no possibility of a successful self-defense, David decided to flee (15:13-14). For the second time in his life, David becomes a fugitive. Behold the misery sin has brought him!

In this valley of humiliation, however, God demonstrated his mercy once again. It came in the form of several loyal servants. These were not "fair weather friends." They were tried and true (cf. Pro. 17:17).

Affirming their unswerving loyalty to David, they told the humbled monarch, *"Behold, thy servants are ready to do whatsoever my lord the king shall appoint"* (15:15). What strong emotion and comfort their faithful love must have been to David's heart!

Ittai's Friendship

Ittai the Gittite is the first to express an unflinching commitment to David (15:19-22). This "stranger" from Gath was willing to jeopardize his own safety and prosperity rather than abandon his loyalty to David. He vowed, *"...whether in death or life, even there also will thy servant be"* (v. 21).

Zadok's Integrity

The priest Zadok and the Levitical priests also went with David. So committed were they to the king God had established that they carried the ark of the covenant with them over the brook Kidron (15:24). Humbly, however, David entreated Zadok to carry the ark back into the city where it belonged.

"If I shall find favor in the eyes of the Lord," David told him, *"He will bring me again, and show me both it [the ark] and His habitation [the tabernacle]: But if he thus say, I have no delight in thee; behold, here am I, let Him do to me as seemeth good unto Him"* (vs. 25-26). What a wonderful spirit of quiet resignation to the sovereignty of God!

Zadok obeyed the king, putting his commitment to God even before his attachment to David. That's integrity! From his proximate position to the throne, however, he would act as an informant to the king (15:28). What a mercy to have the fellowship of such a devoted servant of God!

Hushai's Empathy

As David ascended the mount of Olives, the pathetic king stopped to pray: *"O Lord, I pray thee, turn the counsel of Ahithophel into foolishness"* (15:30-31). The content of his prayer is expressed in Psalm 64, a psalm he likely penned when he received the news that Ahithophel had joined Absalom's rebellion.

No sooner had he reached the top of the mountain, Hushai the Archite came to meet him *"with his coat rent, and earth upon his head"* (v. 32). His dramatic display of grief demonstrated his commitment to David. He identified with David in his humiliation, saying in effect, "Your sorrow is my sorrow." Again, that's true friendship.

David saw in Hushai an answer to his prayer. He asked his "friend" (v. 37) to return to Jerusalem and offer himself as servant to Absalom. By his God-given wisdom, he could *"defeat the counsel of Ahithophel"* for David (vs. 34-36). He willingly obeyed.

David's Prayer

As the king fled from his rebel son, he experienced, as we have seen, the blessing of faithful friendship. His greatest source of strength and comfort, however, was the faithfulness of God.

To that God he turned in his brokenness and distress. His prayer is recorded in Psalm 143. It is a penitential psalm to which everyone who journeys in the valley of humiliation because of their own sins may resort to find expression for their wounded souls. David's greatest "friend" was Jehovah. This Friend would never be untrue to him.

Psalm 143

A Psalm of David.

Hear my prayer, O Lord, give ear to my supplications:
in thy faithfulness answer me, and in thy righteousness.
And enter not into judgment with thy servant:
for in thy sight shall no man living be justified.
For the enemy hath persecuted my soul; he hath smitten my life down to the ground; he hath made me to dwell in darkness, as those that have been long dead.
Therefore is my spirit overwhelmed within me;
my heart within me is desolate.
I remember the days of old; I meditate on all thy works;
I muse on the work of thy hands.
I stretch forth my hands unto thee:
my soul thirsteth after thee, as a thirsty land. Selah.
Hear me speedily, O Lord: my spirit faileth: hide not thy face from me,
lest I be like unto them that go down into the pit.
Cause me to hear thy lovingkindness in the morning; for in thee do I trust: cause me to know the way wherein I should walk: for I lift up my soul unto thee.
Deliver me, O Lord, from mine enemies:
I flee unto thee to hide me.
Teach me to do thy will; for thou art my God:
Thy spirit is good; lead me into the land of uprightness.
Quicken me, O Lord, for thy name's sake:
For thy righteousness' sake bring my soul out of trouble.
And of thy mercy cut off mine enemies, and destroy all them that afflict my soul: for I am thy servant.

Chapter 28
In the Valley of Humiliation
2 Samuel 15:13-16:23

In his celebrated allegory *Pilgrim's Progress*, John Bunyan depicts the struggles of true Christian experience by vivid portraits of places like the Hill Difficulty, the Slough of Despond, Doubting Castle, the Delectable Mountains, and Vanity Fair. One of the most moving scenes he portrays is Christian's journey through the Valley of Humiliation. Bunyan writes,

> "Then he began to go forward; but Discretion, Piety, Charity, and Prudence would accompany him down to the foot of the hill. So they went on together... Then said Christian, 'As it was difficult coming up, so, so far as I can see, it is dangerous going down.' 'Yes,' said Prudence, 'so it is; for it is hard to matter for a man to go down into the Valley of Humiliation, as thou art now, and to catch no slip by the way; therefore,' said they, 'we are come to accompany thee down the hill.' So he began to go down, but very warily, yet he caught a slip or two. Then I saw in my dream that these good companions when Christian was gone to the bottom of the hill, gave him a loaf of bread, a bottle of wine, and a cluster of raisins...
>
> *While Christian is among his godly friends*
> *Their golden mouths make him sufficient mends*
> *For all his griefs; and when they let him go,*
> *He's clad with northern steel from top to toe.*"

David's "Valley of Humiliation" is recorded in 2 Samuel 15:13 - 16:23. Driven from his throne by his rebel son Absalom, David's descent into the abject existence of a fugitive fleeing for his life is filled with emotion.

Like Christian, David was "hard put to it" in this valley. It is indeed "a hard matter for a man to go down into the Valley of Humiliation."

Further, like Christian, David "caught a slip or two" by the way. But, like Christian again, he had "good companions" and "godly friends" that gave him "bread, wine, and a cluster of raisins." Surely, our merciful Lord will not break the bruised reed or quench the smoking flax, but faithfully gives blessings in the midst of burdens.

David's friends were such blessings from the Lord. The loyalty of Ittai the Gittite, Zadok the Priest, and Hushai the Archite must have provided great solace to David in this his hour of humiliation (15:13-37).

In this narrative concerning David's humiliation is a practical message for others whose lives have been turned upside-down. First, here is a lesson to learn; then, a caution to heed; finally, a truth to remember.

A Lesson to Learn

Self-humbling is the right response to adversity (15:30, 32; 16:5-14)

Who can forget that the Savior, on the night of his betrayal, like David (15:23), also crossed the brook Kidron on his descent into the ultimate "humiliation" of the death of the cross? As the Savior's heart was exceeding sorrowful on that occasion, so was David's on this: *"And David...wept as he went up, and had his head covered, and he went up barefoot"* (15:30).

Arthur Pink astutely observes that "the real key to the whole of this passage is to be found in the state of David's heart. Throughout he is to be viewed as the humble penitent."

Self-humbling is the right response when one must pass through the Valley of Humiliation. His own son had made insurrection against him and his most trusted counselor, Ahithophel, had joined Absalom's revolution (15:31; cf. Ps. 55:14). But David does not complain against the Almighty. Instead, he "worships" (15:32; Cf. Ps. 3). How exemplary is the scene!

A "man after God's own heart" will bow submissively before the rod of God's correction. He will not complain for the punishment of his sins, but will search and try his ways, then turn again unto the Lord (Lam. 3:39-40).

He will humbly kiss the rod that has smitten him, deeming God's rebuke "a kindness" (Ps. 141:5). No doubt, God's purpose in affliction is often to bring His children to precisely this point of uncomplaining acquiescence and humbleness of mind before Him.

By nature, man resents the blows of Divine chastening. Pride prompts man to "despise the chastening of the Lord" and to rebel in the anger of depression like Cain (Heb. 12:5; Gen. 4:6-7). Only grace can cause one beneath the bitter stroke to say with Eli, *"It is the Lord; let Him do what seemeth Him good"* (1 Sam. 3:18).

Is there a sweeter sight or more profound testimony to the reality of grace than one who bows in humble and quiet submission before God when trouble presses hard upon him?

In this humble frame of mind, David could even bear the most severe censure. Shimei, of the house of Saul, accosted David and his little band of followers as they came to Bahurim (16:5-14). He cursed, threw dirt in the air, and cast stones at David, calling him "a bloody man of Belial" and charging that David was being punished for usurping Saul's throne.

It was a humiliating experience, but David prohibited Abishai from silencing the man. In fact, he said, *"Let him alone and let him curse, for the Lord hath bidden him"* (vs. 11).

When one smarts under a sense of the justice of God, he is wise to humbly consider each misfortune as something that God has sent for the purpose of teaching His child the heinousness of sin. Though others could see only the outrageous conduct of one of the king's enemies, David discerned the hand of God in this humiliating episode.

He could well bear the frown of Shimei, for he saw in it the frown of God. Likewise, we would do well to humbly consider the possibility of God's displeasure in those seasons when we meet with nothing but opposition.

Even though Shimei was wrong to accuse David (Ex. 22:28; Ecc. 10:20), and even though it was a false accusation, yet David saw the occasion as another evidence of Divine displeasure. He knew that the blood of Saul was not on his hands; but he also knew that the blood of Uriah was!

When men presume to know why we are suffering, let us not react first in self-defense, but examine ourselves to see whether or not there is some merit to the insinuation that the Lord has been offended by us.

Even in the shame of this experience, David comforted himself in the prospect of God's mercy: *"It may be that the Lord will look on mine affliction, and...will requite me good for his cursing this day"* (16:12). The humble suppliant still trusts in the mercy of God. Blessed faith!

A Caution to Heed

Be aware of the tendency to make faulty judgments when the pressure on you is great (16:1-4)

In those seasons when we must travel in the Valley of Humiliation, we must not only respond to Divine chastening with a humble heart, but also be careful to keep a clear and judicious head. Sadly, like Bunyan's "pilgrim," David here suffered "a slip or two."

Taking the occasion of David's adversity to advance his own interests, Ziba, Mephibosheth's servant, met David's company with two asses loaded with food. Ziba had long resented his appointment as servant to the lame-footed grandson of Saul and now saw an opportunity to break free from that ignoble charge.

When David inquired about Mephibosheth, Ziba lied, *"He is at Jerusalem, for he said, 'Today shall the house of Israel restore me the kingdom of my father"* (16:3). Hastily and without investigation, David disinherited Mephibosheth and gave all his substance to Ziba.

It appeared that Ziba was another friend to the unhappy king, but in fact, he was behaving hypocritically. Ziba was exploiting David's distress to his own advantage.

No doubt, David had forgotten that judgment based on hearsay is untrustworthy: *"He that is first in his own cause seemeth just, but his neighbor cometh and searcheth him."* He had forgotten that "charity thinketh no evil."

How frequently those who feel mistreated react uncharitably to every alleged detractor! *"Judge not according to outward appearances,"* says John 7:24, *"but judge righteous judgment,"* lest afterward we bitterly regret our hasty decisions.

A Truth to Remember
When truth is on the scaffold and wrong is on the throne, God stands somewhere in the shadows, keeping watch above His own (16:15-23)

Chapter sixteen concludes with the account of Hushai in Absalom's presence. He was there not because he sympathized with the revolution, but at David's command, if perchance he might be able to overthrow the counsel of Ahithophel.

A peek ahead into the narrative reveals that the plan was in fact successful: *"For the Lord had appointed to defeat the good counsel of Ahithophel, to the intent that the Lord might bring evil upon Absalom"* (17:14).

May this lesson teach us that during those moments when it seems that God has allowed evil to triumph, He is in fact at work behind the scenes, for the good of His people and the glory of His great name. Though "wrong" is on the throne of Jerusalem, God is on the throne of Heaven. Such a reminder of His sovereignty is essential to those who pass, albeit for the moment, through the Valley of Humiliation.

Chapter 29
The Rebellion Put Down by God
2 Samuel 16:15 - 18:18

God is a covenant keeper and although at the moment his chastening rod was on David, his covenant with David was permanent. He had sworn once and for all and would not lie: *"Thy seed will I establish forever, and build up thy throne to all generations"* (Ps. 89:3-4, 34-35). This unilateral and unconditional promise meant that God would never ultimately forsake David, regardless of David's faithfulness.

Jehovah's covenant loyalty to David, then, is the theological basis of 2 Samuel 17-18. Why did the Lord discomfit David's enemies and sabotage the conspiracy to take the throne at the very moment David was under Divine discipline? Because He had pledged Himself in covenant commitment to David, and God cannot lie.

In His sovereign providence, God put down Absalom's insurrection. He dismantled the rebel forces from the inside. He was the saboteur that overturned the revolution. Through a series of natural and ordinary events, God worked to confuse the issues, to protect David's informants, to care for the indigents, and to catch the leader of the revolution himself.

God Confuses Absalom's Mind

Providence is the theological word to describe how God intervenes in the ordinary circumstances of life to influence the outcome according to His will. Second Samuel 17:1-14 is a classic example of providence.

Ahithophel counseled Absalom to attack David *"while he is weary and weak handed"* (v. 2). David's soldiers,

Ahithophel predicted, will flee, David will be smitten, and all the people of Israel will rally around Absalom as their uncontested king. It seemed that Ahithophel had a case.

But when Hushai was consulted, he advised that Ahithophel's counsel was not timely (v. 7). *"Thy father is a mighty man and a man of war,"* he said. "Furthermore, they are currently seeking revenge, like a bear bereaved of her whelps. He's too experienced to lodge with the people," he added (v. 8).

Instead of Ahithophel's planned attack, Hushai advised Absalom to wait until he had gathered a large army, then to personally lead his troops in an ambush (vs. 11-12). With a more unified effort, he said, no fortress could withstand the attack (v. 13).

Absalom said, *"The counsel of Hushai...is better than the counsel of Ahithophel. For the Lord had appointed to defeat the good counsel of Ahithophel, to the intent that the Lord might bring evil upon Absalom"* (v. 14). The God who holds every man's heart in his hand can turn their thoughts like rivers of water whithersoever He wills (Pro. 21:1).

God Protects David's Informants

Hushai then sent word to David, *"Don't pitch your camp tonight in the plains of the wilderness, but speedily pass over Jordan, for Ahithophel has encouraged Absalom to overtake you as your troops rest"* (vs. 15-16). The message was relayed by Zadok and Abiathar to a wench (lit. a female slave) who told Jonathan and Ahimaaz who were dispatched to tell David (vs. 15-17). A young boy, however, saw as the wench gave the information to them and ran to tell Absalom.

Knowing that they had been discovered, Jonathan and Ahimaaz stopped at a man's house in Bahurim. The man's wife hid them in the well, put a covering over its mouth, and spread ground corn on top.

When Absalom's servants inquired about the two informants, their search was disappointed and they returned to Jerusalem. The two informants then completed their mission and David's men escaped safely across Jordan (vs. 18-22).

When Ahithophel saw that his counsel had been disregarded, he took his own life (v. 23). Again, in this ordinary course of events God superintended the circumstances to overthrow the wicked devices of men.

God Shows Mercy to David's Soldiers

As David came to Mahanaim, Absalom's army crossed the Jordan and pitched in the land of Gilead (vs. 24-26). Meanwhile in Mahanaim, three more of David's supporters, Shobi, Machir, and Barzillai, brought lavish supplies to David's troops, including beds, hygiene items, vegetables, breads, meat, and desserts, *"for they said, The people is hungry, and weary, and thirsty, in the wilderness"* (v. 27-29).

Who put compassion into the hearts of these strangers (one Ammonite and two transjordanian Gileadites) toward David? The God who holds the hearts of all men in his hand! In humble gratitude for God's mercy, David here composed Psalms 61 and 62.

God Captures Absalom in an Oak

Refreshed at Mahanaim, David gathered his army together and prepared to meet Absalom's army in battle (18:1-4). But once again, David allowed parental sentiment to overrule kingly judgment: *"Deal gently for my sake with the young man, even with Absalom,"* he commanded Joab (18:5).

As the battle began, David's servants fought brilliantly so that there was a great slaughter of twenty-thousand of Absalom's men that day. Strangely enough, however, the narrative records that *"the wood [i.e. the forest of Ephraim] devoured more people that day than the sword devoured"* (v. 8). What is this but another indication of Divine providence?

Then, as Absalom rode to meet the servants of David, his mule took him under the thick boughs of a great oak tree. Absalom's long hair "caught hold" of the tree. He was pulled from his mount and suspended by his hair in the oak (vs. 9). When he was made aware of the young renegade's plight, Joab shot three arrows through his heart as he hung from the oak by his hair (vs. 10-18).

Behind the scenes of this sequence of events, God stands in the shadows, discomfiting the plans of his enemies, showing mercy to His servants, and squashing every attempt to overthrow his purposes, because His covenant will not be broken.

Absalom imagined that his assault was against David. Had it been so, he would have been victorious. But Absalom was striving against God. Such a foolish campaign cannot succeed.

Psalm 61

To the chief Musician upon Neginah, A Psalm of David

¹Hear my cry, O God; attend unto my prayer.
²From the end of the earth will I cry unto thee,
when my heart is overwhelmed:
lead me to the rock that is higher than I.
³For thou hast been a shelter for me,

and a strong tower from the enemy.
⁴I will abide in thy tabernacle for ever:
I will trust in the covert of thy wings. Selah.
⁵For thou, O God, hast heard my vows:
thou hast given me the heritage of those that fear thy name.
⁶Thou wilt prolong the king's life:
and his years as many generations.
⁷He shall abide before God for ever:
O prepare mercy and truth,
which may preserve him.
⁸So will I sing praise unto thy name for ever,
that I may daily perform my vows.

Chapter 30
Coming Home
2 Samuel 18:19-19:39

Throughout the inspired biography of David, he appears at times as a man driven by principle. He was indeed a man of character with strong convictions of what was righteous in the sight of God.

At other times, however, he is driven by passion and sentiment. He was a man of strong emotion. It seems to me that his best moments were those occasions when he was ruled by his head, and his worst, when he allowed emotion to dictate his actions.

This balanced presentation of his psyche makes him thoroughly real to us. We can identify with this struggle between principle and passion, between conviction and emotion, character and personality—between the head and the heart, for David's conflict, like ours, was precipitated by a dual nature described by Paul as "the flesh" and "the spirit" (Rom. 7; Gal. 5).

At times, as the passage before us indicates, David exhibits noble and exemplary virtues. At other times, he displays the vices of a fallen, depraved nature. Let's peer once more into the very heart and soul of this intriguing man.

A Broken Heart (18:19 - 19:7)

We find the aged monarch anxiously waiting for tidings from the battlefield. He had urged his generals to *"deal gently with the young man Absalom, for my sake."* Now, his only concern as the courier draws near is the safety of his rebel child: *"Is the young man Absalom safe?"* (18:32).

The Ethiopian courier Cushi replied, *"The enemies of my lord the king, and all that rise against thee to do thee hurt, be as that young man."* Overwhelmed with grief at these words, David retires to his chamber and begins to weep aloud: *"O my son, Absalom! My son, my son, Absalom! Would God I had died for thee, O Absalom, my son, my son!"* (18:33).

Who can fault David for this excessive response? It was a parental sorrow, filled with the deep emotions that only a parent feels for a child. Further, it was just one more tragedy added to the pile of burdens that had afflicted him in the wake of his terrible sin.

Amnon, his firstborn, the infant child of Bathsheba, and now Absalom - three of his sons were dead in a matter of a few years. It is indeed hard to feel anything but the deepest sympathy for David at this moment.

But David had allowed emotion to overrule conviction. We want to challenge him, "Have you forgotten that Absalom was the leader of the rebellion against your own throne?" Would Absalom have spared the life of David if the roles were reversed?

David's sorrow cast a depressing pall over all his soldiers: *"The victory that day was turned into mourning unto all the people"* (19:2). Krummacher writes, "To the army, to whom the rebel Absalom had become an object of deepest abhorrence, and who saw in his death nothing less than a glorifying of the retributive justice of Jehovah, the sorrow to which the king abandoned himself seemed unmanly, and a forgetting of God: and when they perceived that their commander-in-chief refrained not...they became at length weary...and were on the point of quitting the field and scattering, every man to his home."

Joab finally went to David, accusing him of *"loving his enemies and hating his friends"* because he mourned for the slain rebel and shunned recognition to the faithful soldiers who had risked all for him. He counseled David to compose himself and speak to his troops, else he risked losing the loyalty of his only remaining servants (19:1-7).

A Gallant Heart (19:8-14)

With a new perspective on the events of the day, David gathered his composure and gallantly made a public appearance. As the news spread that the king was sitting in the gate of Mahanaim, the people emerged from their tents with a new optimism and sense of purpose.

No doubt, David's heart was still filled with sadness, but the responsibilities of leadership required strength of character. For the welfare of "the sheep" he had been called to shepherd, David nobly put public duty above personal distress.

Meanwhile, back in Jerusalem, tensions among the people of Israel surfaced. Someone asked, "Why is no one talking about bringing the king back? Absalom is dead and David was a wonderful king. Why should we hesitate to restore him to the throne?" (19:9-10).

As news reached David that the pendulum of public opinion had swung back in his favor, he sent to the elders of Judah asking the same question: "Why do you delay to restore the kingdom to me?" His speech was so compelling that a large delegation was appointed to conduct the king back to his rightful home (19:11-15).

A Forgiving Heart (19:15-23)

At the head of this delegation was Shimei, the man who had cursed the already humiliated king the day he was deposed from the throne. Shimei fell before David and confessed: *"Let not my lord impute iniquity unto me, neither do thou remember that which thy servant did perversely the day that my lord the king went out of Jerusalem, that the king should take it to his heart. For thy servant doth know that I have sinned..."* (19:19-20).

Abishai, remembering with indignation the humiliating episode, again wants Shimei put to death. But David mercifully says, *"No man shall be put to death this day in Israel."* And David pardoned Shimei (19:21-23).

Was Shimei genuinely penitent? Who can tell? The narrative gives us no reason to doubt it. The most notable thing is not Shimei's confession, but David's renewed mastery of his spirit. The narrative focuses on that.

Knowing that he is the recipient of God's free grace, David exercise amazing self-control of his natural impulse to retaliate, allowing conviction to rule passion. The mercy he extends to the man responsible for such an injustice is indeed marvelous.

A Calloused Heart (19:24-30)

But no sooner had he exhibited such piety of character, but David once again allows the old man to mar the lovely scene. Prejudice blinds him as he lifts his eyes from Shimei to see another who had come to conduct him home—Mephibosheth.

Mephibosheth was a pitiful sight. Since the day David left, he had not bathed, shaved, or changed the bandages on his crippled feet. Did not his very appearance bespeak his devotion to the king, contrary to Ziba's incriminating accusation that David had accepted so readily?

But if the question crossed his mind, David pushed it aside. *"Why didn't you go with me, Mephibosheth?"* David asked. David's duplicity in mourning for a rebel and pardoning a slanderer while now insinuating that he suspected the crippled Mephibosheth as a traitor is unbecoming to such a pious and spiritual man. But again, David has permitted passion (in this case, the passion of prejudice) to rule reason.

Mephibosheth answered, "I wanted to and planned to, but when I asked Ziba to prepare the ass for my transportation, he left without me." He then added, *"And he hath slandered thy servant unto my lord the king; but my lord the king is as an angel of God: do therefore what is good in thine eyes...What right have I yet to cry any more unto the king?"* (19:24-28).

One would think that his humble posture alone would convince David that he had been fooled by Ziba. Did David then apologize to Mephibosheth for disinheriting him? Did he ask forgiveness for believing the worst?

No, he callously said, "I'm tired of hearing about this. You and Ziba divide the land." Where is his mercy now? Where is his sense of what is just and right and honorable? It is obscured by his pride and prejudice! Alas, the tragedy of a calloused heart!

As further evidence of his sincerity and nobility of character, the lame-footed son of Jonathan said, *"Yea, let him take all, forasmuch as my lord the king is come again in peace unto his own house"* (19:30). The only thing that mattered to Mephibosheth is that the one who had been so gracious to him was now back where he belonged. Ah, the nobility of a humble heart!

This episode reminds us that the best of men are but men at their very best. Even great servants of God like David made miscalculations and failed to judge righteous judgment in every case.

A Grateful Heart (19:31-39)

Once again, after this momentary stumble on his way home, however, David displays the virtues of the new nature. The eighty-year-old Barzillai, who had sustained him at Mahanaim, walked with him over Jordan.

Suddenly, David's heart was filled with gratitude for all that this aged gentleman had done for him. "Come live in the palace," David said to him. But Barzillai said, "I'm old. I would only be a burden." He then stated his intention of traveling with the king a little way over Jordan, then returning to live out the rest of his days at his own home.

He indicated, however, that if David was intent on showing gratitude to him, he could convey the honor on another in his place. David gladly agreed to his elderly friend's request and told Barzillai that in addition to that, anything else he wanted, he would gladly do it (19:31-38).

As they crossed Jordan, David embraced the old man and blessed him. Barzillai turned back to Mahanaim and David continued with a grateful heart on his long-awaited journey home.

Chapter 31
Yet Another Revolt
2 Samuel 19:40 - 20:26

When passions have been raised to a fevered pitch, they do not soon subside. Though Absalom's rebellion has been squashed and the king escorted back to his rightful throne, the frenzy of "warring madness" still stirs among the people.

The task of rebuilding the government from the wreckage of Absalom's revolution would not be easy, and it didn't take long for the Adversary to stir the smoldering embers of animosity from the ashes of the former conflict once again.

Sheba's Sedition

As the "welcome home" delegation made its way to Jerusalem, the men of Judah were met by representatives from the ten tribes of Israel (19:41). They felt that they had been slighted because they were not included in the proceedings. Pretending that they desired to see the king honored, the men of Israel expressed offense at the omission. Clearly, they were insulted.

The men of Judah, however, did not respond in a godly way. Fiercely, they retorted, *"The king is near of kin to us"* (19:42). The men of Israel replied, "We have more rights to the crown because we have ten tribes, and you have only two" (19:43). And so the childish quarrel concerning "who loved David the most" continued.

Just at this point, while the contention smoldered, Sheba, a man of Belial, blew a trumpet and uttered words that sparked the combustion of revolution. *"We have no* part in David," he ventured, "*neither have we inheritance in the son of Jesse: every man to his tents, O Israel*" (20:1).

The interest the men of Israel had expressed in David now showed its true colors, for all Israel followed Sheba, leaving David to return to Jerusalem to resume his reign over a divided kingdom. Sadly, few people think for themselves, especially in the heat of the moment, but follow blindly the mob spirit.

Two practical principles emerge from this episode: *(1) The new conflict on the heels of the other should serve to remind us that there is nothing stable in this world and we can only expect to be disappointed if we build our hopes on man or the world.*

The individual whose expectations for happiness are rooted in his circumstances or in the people around him is sure to be disillusioned. Only the Lord will never disappoint us. The further one travels down the road in this journey of life, the sweeter is the prospect of a world where there is no more conflict.

(2) When God's people allow selfish pride and jealousy to surface, Satan capitalizes on the situation to foster disunity and division. The contention and strife between the men of Judah and the men of Israel provided fertile soil for the seeds of mutiny and discord.

A. W. Pink writes, "Satan knows full well that few things are better calculated to further his own base designs than by causing division among the people of God." How important it is then to mortify the flesh, to die to foolish pride and ego in all our dealings with one another. Christians should labor to be as inclusive as possible, opting to separate only when doctrinal purity is jeopardized.

Joab's Jealousy

Knowing that time was of the essence, David charged Amasa, whom he had commissioned to replace Joab, to gather the men of Judah to overthrow Sheba's rebellion (20:1ff). He gave him three days to assemble the army, most of whom had retired to their own personal concerns in the wake of the crisis in leadership. This was no small task, for Amasa had allied himself to Absalom and would, no doubt, be held suspect among Joab's soldiers.

When he didn't return in the three days David had appointed, he began to suspect that Amasa had defected to Sheba. With no time to waste, David was obliged to consult with Abishai (and through him, no doubt, to assign the task of overthrowing Sheba's revolt to Joab).

As they came to the great stone at Gibeon, Amasa arrived. Sensing that this, his traitorous cousin, was David's choice to supplant him, Joab, driven by his own jealousy, seized the opportunity to slay his rival Amasa (20:9-13).

Finally, with the confused army once again assembled under Joab, the errand was resumed. They made their way to Abel where Sheba had fled.

Joab and his men began their assault upon the city until a "wise woman" called unto Joab from the wall. Respectfully, he listened as she reminded the general that Abel was a city held in reputation for its wise counsel.

Joab had failed to inquire whether or not the town sympathized with Sheba. To destroy the entire town would be to work folly in Israel, she urged. Joab replied, *"Far be it from me that I should destroy the city. Deliver Sheba only and I will depart"* (20:16-21).

This wise woman then explained the situation to the inhabitants of the city and Sheba's head was thrown to

Joab over the wall. Their mission complete, Joab and his men returned to David in Jerusalem.

Joab is indeed an intriguing character. The whole of his history indicates that he was an unprincipled man of fierce temper, arrogant and matchless spirit, and reckless and brutal behavior. He would stop at nothing to advance his own interests. Yet, strangely, he was not himself a threat to the throne of the king. He did not aspire to rebel against David's throne, but neither did he hesitate to guard his own interests.

Further, Joab was, on more than one occasion, respectfully submissive to the counsel of "wise women." He is indeed an enigma.

Perhaps the best parallel to Joab would be the man in the world who appears to be very moral and upright, but whose morality is motivated not by love to God or neighbor, but by a pragmatic love of self. At first we might admire Joab's loyalty to David, his tenacious work ethic, and his readiness to submit to wise counsel. Then, it becomes apparent that Joab's morality is a mere sham, for it is not motivated by love for God but concern for self.

David's attempt to once and for all replace the ruthless Joab had been foiled, though the campaign to squash the new rebellion had been successful. Once again, the king was on his throne. And once again, *"Joab was over all the host of Israel"* (v. 23).

The consequences of David's great sin would be with him the rest of his life. Never again would David know unalloyed happiness. But then, never again would he experience unmitigated trouble. Absalom and Sheba were gone, but Joab would not seem to go away. Thankfully, however, neither would the Lord his God.

Chapter 32
The Justice of David's God
2 Sam. 21 & 24

A W. Tozer wrote, "There is plenty of good news in the Bible, but there is never any flattery or back scratching." David's story, especially in the aftermath of his great sin, is a prime illustration of that fact.

The dominant tone of the narrative from 2 Samuel 11 to the end of David's life is one of severity. The Divine attribute shining most clearly is God's justice, not His love—God's government, not His grace.

Perhaps that is the reason so little attention is paid to this segment of David's biography. Man's fallen nature recoils at the thought of Divine judgment. But this portion of the narrative of David's life was included by the Holy Spirit, I am convinced, to force us to face the subject toward which we possess such a passionate natural allergy.

On the same principle that the introduction of a small amount of the polio or flu virus immunizes a patient against contracting the disease, so the act of facing a subject that brings us the most discomfort vaccinates the believer from a distorted view of God and of life.

David himself, as the sacred history demonstrates, frequently allowed sentiment to control principle. The mercy he extended to Absalom, for instance, and to Amasa, was not genuine mercy at all, for it bypassed the principles of righteousness. It was rather sheer human sentimentality.

God's mercy is never extended at the expense of justice. To overlook sin would not be a virtue in God, but a moral imperfection. Thus, at the close of his life, the two final trials with which David meets are, once again, sobering and shocking reminders that God is Just.

If a godly man like David needed further sanctification in his view of God—that is, if God thought it best to correct the imbalance that existed in David's heart and mind by hammering him with two such heavy blows—then who am I to presume that my perception of God is entirely disaffected by my own preconceived biases and presuppositions'? None of us have perfectly the mind of Christ. We don't always affirm what He affirms and deny what He denies.

God deals with us, consequently, like He dealt with David, to teach us to think His thoughts after Him, even if it requires a curriculum that seems unusually severe. It is only through personal trauma that God makes us aware that the tendency to recoil at this aspect of the Divine character is not an intellectual, but a moral aversion.

What two crushing blows composed the final trial that brought the flinching king face to face with the justice of God? (1)A three year famine (2 Sam. 21) and a pestilence (lit. disease) that killed 70,000 Israelites (2 Sam. 24).

The Curse Causeless Shall not Come

The first trial was not the direct result of David's sin, but in fact, of Saul's. David recognized that the lengthy famine was not mere coincidence. He knew the principle that Solomon later framed into words, *"The curse causeless shall not come"* (Pro. 26:2). There was a reason for the absence of rain.

Even though Scripture plainly teaches that every calamity is not the result of direct sin (cf. Book of Job; Jno. 9:2ff), yet it also teaches that sometimes, adversity in life is due to our disobedience. David knew that God communicates both His favor and His displeasure to people via the circumstances of life.

Most people, however, like Israel of old, fail to perceive God's message in calamity, attributing trouble to sheer "fate" or "random chance" or "natural causes." They don't associate their difficulties to their relationship with God.

Amos says that God sent "want of bread," "blasting and mildew," "pestilence and war," and "natural disasters," together with a lengthy drought upon Israel, "yet have ye not returned unto me" (Amos 4:6-11). They didn't get the message. Perhaps they thought it was just *El Nina*, or some phenomenon of nature. David knew, on the contrary, that this particular curse had a cause (cf. 2 Chr. 7:13-14; Hag. 1:5-6).

He inquired, therefore, of the Lord and the Lord replied, *"It is for Saul, and for his bloody house, because he slew the Gibeonites"* (21:1). The Gibeonites had been promised asylum within Israel by Joshua. For four hundred years, they lived peacefully among the people of God, serving the Hebrews as *"drawers of water and hewers of wood."*

But Saul had inflicted upon them an unprovoked and brutal slaughter, violating the treaty made to them in the name of Jehovah (v. 2). This travesty of justice cried out for expiation, and, as David now learned, was the cause for the grievous famine upon the land.

Two practical principles emerge from this lesson: (1) Learn that actions today may have consequences on future generations; (2) Learn that God is just and will permit no injustice to go unrequited.

Forced to face the consequences of Saul's sins (just as others had been forced to live in the consequences of David's sin), David asked the Gibeonites what should be done. They replied, *"Let seven sons of Saul be delivered unto us and we will hang them up unto the Lord in Gibeah of Saul"* (v. 6).

No doubt, with a conflict between his sense of justice and his gentle temperament, David agreed to the terms. He was learning that regardless of the inner turmoil he felt, he must submit humbly to the God whose ways are just and righteous altogether. Surely God intends in all things to be recognized and revered as Holy and Just.

A precious scene is recorded that displays a beautiful spirit of submission before God's justice. Rizpah, the mother of two of the victims, covered their bodies with sackcloth and guarded them against bird and beast, waiting for the rain to return on the land (v. 10). Smarting, no doubt, under the blow of Divine justice upon her personal life, she yet humbly looked for the end of the three year drought that this act of expiation would bring to God's people.

So touched was David by her godly response, he gathered the remains of all seven victims and buried them royally, with the bones of Saul and Jonathan in the sepulcher of Kish, Saul's father (v. 14). *"And after that God was entreated for the land."*

Krummacher writes, "One may conceive what David must have suffered in his soul on account of that judicial act. That terrible execution ran directly counter to his whole disposition. But to him, who more than once had exercised unseasonable clemency instead of righteousness, it could not but be for his advantage, to see himself confronted by so imposing a display of the righteousness of God."

David's Sinful Census (2 Sam. 24)

The story of David concludes with yet another episode reinforcing the justice of God. This time, the judgments that fell upon Israel were the direct result of David's sin— namely, His sinful pride.

The "he" of 2 Samuel 24:1 is clearly "Satan," as 1 Chronicles 21:1 indicates. Satan tempted David to number Israel, no doubt, by suggesting thoughts of pride to his mind.

The renewed unification of the people gave David a sense of relief and satisfaction. Surely, we are happy for him to know that Israel is once again proceeding apace and prospering under his scepter. But Satan is subtle. He likes to capitalize on a situation in which one is content, either to make him lazy or to make him proud. In the case of David's sin with Bathsheba, prosperity made him lazy. On this occasion, prosperity has made him proud.

Even against Joab's objection, David persisted to take his self-appointed census. How foolish he was not to heed the propitious warning, God's "escape hatch" from this temptation (cf. 1 Cor. 10:13)!

The census took nine and one-half months, but the results were impressive: 1,300,000 soldiers in David's army (vs. 8-9). Suddenly, when the results were tallied, David knew he had done wrong. His heart smote him and he prayed for forgiveness (v. 10). It is always our own fault when we allow ourselves to be deceived by Satan.

The next morning, the prophet Gad approached the king with a message from the Lord. The Lord offered David three options concerning the consequence of his sin: seven years of famine, three months of military defeat, or three days of pestilence (v. 13).

One might ask, if David confessed and prayed for forgiveness, why did the Lord still execute judgment? Because He is just! Mercy, again, is never extended at the expense of justice.

Yes, God is faithful and just to forgive the sin of those who penitently confess all, but God's grace does not revoke God's government. David, as well as we, needed to learn that lesson.

The options were basically two. He could either suffer at the hands of God (through famine or pestilence) or at the hands of man (through war). Whatever God might choose, whether seven years of famine or three days of an epidemic disease, would be better than falling into the hands of man, David reasoned. *"Let us fall now into the hand of the Lord; for his mercies are great: and let me not fall into the hand of man"* (v. 14).

David understood that God is good, as well as severe (Rom. 11:22). Even in the midst of Divine chastening, the sinner's only hope is to rely still upon his sovereign mercy (cf. Lam. 3:32-34).

God's mercy was indeed demonstrated in the option He selected, i.e. the 3 days of disease over the 7 years of famine. The pestilence raced through the land, killing 70,000 people over the course of three days. When the angel came to Jerusalem however, Jehovah said, *"It is enough; stay now thine hand."*

At the sight of the angel, David was deeply humbled. He cried out, *"I have sinned, and I have done wickedly: but these sheep, what have they done'? Let thine hand, I pray thee, be against me, and against my father's house"* (vs. 15-17). His willingness to sacrifice himself for the people of God is indeed lovely.

At Gad's instruction, David purchased the threshing floor of Araunah the Jebusite, erected an altar unto the Lord there, and offered burnt offerings and peace offerings unto the Lord. So the plague was stayed (vs. 18-25).

It was this sacrifice alone, an atonement that God had prescribed in the law of Moses, which satisfied the justice of God. And the seraphim raised the antiphonal chorus, "Holy, Holy, Holy is the Lord God of hosts." And David said 'amen.'

Chapter 33
Dwelling in the House of the Lord Forever
1 Chronicles 28-29

"God buries His workmen," said John Wesley, "but carries on His work." The work is His and the ministries He gives to men are but temporary stewardships, not personal franchises. David knew that he was only a small part of the larger picture that would continue to unfold even after he was gone. How refreshing it is, therefore, to see him in his final days making plans toward the future!

Preparing God's People for the Future (28:1-10)

David desired to communicate his vision concerning the building of the temple in such a way that it would become the common cause of the people. To this end, he gathered a national assembly and rehearsed for them God's sovereignty in the selection of a king (vs. 4-6).

He reminded them of the importance of obeying God's word that the kingdom be established forever and that they might enjoy the blessings of the land God had given them (vs. 7-8). Finally, he admonished Solomon to be diligent and courageous in the task to which God had called him (vs. 9-10).

All in all, it is a moving charge in which David publicly reminded the people of their noble opportunities to glorify God by serving Him with a perfect heart and a willing mind.

Providing for God's House in the Future (28:11-29:9)

David then gave to Solomon the building plans for the future temple, plans that had been communicated to David by God (v. 12). He also delivered to him the building materials accrued such as gold and silver for the construction of the various items of furniture.

Then he continued his charge: *"Be strong, and of good courage and do it: fear not, nor be dismayed: for the Lord God, even my God, will be with thee; he will not fail thee, nor forsake thee, until thou hast finished all the work for the service of the house of the Lord"* (v. 20).

The task before Solomon was especially significant and David deemed it an honor to participate in even the preparatory stages. His commitment to and zeal for the house of God is a wonderful example to all today who serve the Lord Jesus Christ.

Whether he would be present to witness the happy day or not, David was concerned to honor his Lord by giving of his personal substance for the future temple (29:3). He *"set his affection to the house of his God"* (29:3) and *"prepared with all his might for"* it (29:2).

Then David turned to the congregation for the purpose of enforcing the importance of this great work: *"Solomon my son, whom alone God hath chosen, is yet young and tender, and the work is great: for the palace is not for man, but for the Lord God"* (29:1). He asked, *"Who then is willing to consecrate his service this day unto the Lord?"* (v. 5).

Compelled by the noble aim, the people offered willingly (v. 6). They gave gold, silver, brass, iron, and precious jewels. *"Then the people rejoiced for that they offered willingly, because with perfect heart they offered willingly to the Lord: and David the king also rejoiced with great joy"* (v. 9).

Praying for God's Blessing on the Future (29:10-20)

David's joy expressed itself in a prayer of thanksgiving before the whole congregation in which he gives all the glory to the Lord. *"Thine O Lord is the greatness, and the power, and the glory, and the victory, and the majesty"* (v.11). The gifts the people had offered, David acknowledges, were blessings God had given them in the first place, and blessings they were happy, even privileged (29:14), to return to His service.

In verse 15-16, he confesses the transitory nature of this life and consequently, the insignificance of accumulating material possessions when compared with the noble goal of building a house for the glory of God's holy name.

Then he prays that God would help His people to always remember the preciousness of His house and prepare their hearts to serve Him (v. 18). He also prays for Solomon, that God would give him a perfect heart to keep His commandments (v. 19). Then David and the entire congregation worshipped the Lord.

Passing God's Crown to the Future King (29:21-25)

For the next two days, the people sacrificed to the Lord a thousand bullocks, a thousand rams, and a thousand lambs. There was great joy in Israel.

Then Solomon was inaugurated king, and the people bowed before him as they had previously submitted to David. It was evident to all that God had bestowed on him unprecedented royal majesty (vs. 22-25).

What a blessing it must have been to David to witness God's blessings upon Solomon and the people of Israel! Surely now he could die in peace.

Praising God's Name Forever (29:26-30)

And die he did. God buried his workman David, but God carried on His work in the world through Solomon.

David was content to leave God's house here for God's house in heaven. His work of shepherding Israel had been completed. Now it was time for him to dwell in the house of the Lord forever (Ps. 23:6). The divine work of his education was over. The glorious day of his eternal rest was now begun.

www.ingramcontent.com/pod-product-compliance
Lightning Source LLC
Chambersburg PA
CBHW020803160426
43192CB00006B/419